ENTITIES &
FRAGMENTS

KEYS TO THE KINGDOM SERIES
POCKET EDITION

THIS BOOK SHOULD NOT BE LEFT
ACCESSIBLE, IN CLEAR VIEW, OR
SHARED CASUALLY WITH OTHERS

Published from
Mardukite Borsippa HQ, San Luis Valley, Colorado
Mardukite Academy & Systemology Society
for spiritual or philosophical purposes only

ENTITIES & FRAGMENTS

Systemology
Advanced Training Course
Manual #5

As presented by Joshua Free
to the Systemology Society

© 2024, JOSHUA FREE

ISBN : 978-1-961509-52-8

This manual is restricted to students on
The Systemology Advanced Training Course
that have already completed the
"Pathway to Ascension" Professional Course

References to prerequisite material:
"The Secret of Universes" (AT #1)
"Games, Goals & Purposes" (AT #2)
"The Jewel of Knowledge" (AT #3)
"Implanted Universes" (AT #4)
Processing-Levels 0 to 4 (PC-1 to 10)
"Spiritual Implants" (PC-11)
"Games & Universes" (PC-12)
"Spiritual Energy" (PC-13)
"Spiritual Machinery" (PC-14)

Full use of this manual may also require:
"Systemology Biofeedback"
"Systemology Procedures" and
"Systemology Piloting"

First Edition Pocket Paperback — *March 2024*

mardukite.com

The Keys to the Kingdom are Yours for the Taking!

The official Mardukite Systemology "Advanced Training Course" is now available in print for the first time.

Those Seekers that have completed the "Pathway to Ascension" Systemology Professional Course can now access the upper-level teachings of our tradition.

This book is not for everyone...
This is the first manual for Level-8.

Never before has Joshua Free presented this material outside the confines of the Mardukite NexGen Systemology Society.

Learn how to expertly apply our spiritual technology toward reaching higher levels of Awareness and Beingness than ever before thought possible for humanity on planet Earth.

Each of the "Keys to the Kingdom" Advanced Training Course Manuals will further a Seekers reach on the Pathway leading out of this Universe.

Systemology Biofeedback
Systemology Procedures
Systemology Piloting

TABLET OF CONTENTS

INTRODUCTION TO THE MANUAL

A.T. MANUAL #5:
ENTITIES & FRAGMENTS

APPENDIX

Advanced Manuals should be studied in the sequential order in which they are numbered.

INTRODUCTION TO
THE MANUAL

This manual is restricted to students on
The Systemology Advanced Training Course
that have already completed the
"Pathway to Ascension" Professional Course

References to prerequisite material:
"The Secret of Universes" (AT #1)
"Games, Goals & Purposes" (AT #2)
"The Jewel of Knowledge" (AT #3)
"Implanted Universes" (AT #4)
Processing-Levels 0 to 4 (PC-1 to 10)
"Spiritual Implants" (PC-11)
"Games & Universes" (PC-12)
"Spiritual Energy" (PC-13)
"Spiritual Machinery" (PC-14)

Full use of this manual may also require:
"Systemology Biofeedback"
"Systemology Procedures" and
"Systemology Piloting"

THE SYSTEMOLOGY ADVANCED TRAINING COURSE MANUAL SERIES

Mardukite Systemology is a new evolution in Human understanding about the "systems" governing *Life*, *Reality*, the *Universe* and all *Existences*. It is also a *Spiritual Path* used to transcend the Human experience and reach *"Ascension."*

This is an *Advanced Training* (*AT*) course manual detailing *upper-levels* of our spiritual philosophy. It is intended to assist *advancing* a *Seeker's* personal progress toward the *upper-most levels* of the *Pathway*.

This manual follows after our *Professional Course* series of lessons—available as individual booklets, or collected in two volumes titled *"The Pathway to Ascension"* The *Professional Course* follows after material given in the *Basic Course* booklets, or *"Fundamentals of Systemology"* volume.

The systematic methodology that we use to assist an individual to increase their *"Actualized Awareness"* (and reach gradually higher toward their *"Spiritual Ascension"*) is referred to as *"The Pathway"* — and that individual is called a *"Seeker."*

To receive the greatest benefit from this manual: it is expected that a *Seeker* will already be familiar with the fundamental concepts and terminology (previously relayed in the *Basic Course* and *Professional Course* lessons) of our *applied philosophy*.

As a *Seeker* increases their *Awareness* in this lifetime, their spiritual *"Knowingness"* also increases—which is to say their *certainty* on *Life*, on this and other *Universes*, and on *realizing Self* as an unlimited "spiritual being" *having* an enforced restrictive "human experience." A *Seeker* also *knowingly* increases their command and control of the "human experience." And this is a part of what is meant by *"Actualized Awareness."*

CHARTING FLIGHTS ON THE PATHWAY

Although there is a systematic structure to *fragmentation,* the personal journey experienced along the *Pathway* will be different for each *Seeker.* For example, certain areas will seem more *"turbulent"* or difficult for one *Seeker* than another. We tend to say that these areas have more *"charge"* on them—or that they are more *"heavily charged."* It is best to handle such areas when you are already feeling "good" and not in a situation (or condition) where that specific area is consistently being *"triggered"* or *"restimulated."*

As an applied philosophy, *Systemology* "theory" can be easily utilized in the "laboratory" of the "world-at-large" in everyday life. This is implied within the basic instruction of each lesson. Unlike other "sciences" that conduct experiments by making a change to some "objective variable" *out there* and waiting to see an effect, our focus is the individual (or *Observer*) themselves, and how *they* affect the *"Reality"* perceived.

Our philosophy is applied by using specific exercises and systematic techniques. These *"processes"* provide the most stable personal gain (and *realizations*) for each area; but only when actually applied with a *Seeker's* full *"presence"* and *Awareness*. Hundreds of such *processes* may be found in the *"Pathway to Ascension"* (*Professional Course*) material.

Applying a technique is called *"running a process."* *Processes* are designed with very simple instructions or *"command-lines."* To *run* a *processing command-line*, a *Seeker* may be assisted by the communication of that *line* from a *"Co-Pilot"* (as in *"Traditional Piloting"*). But even then, a *Seeker* must still personally "input" the *command* as *Self*. For this reason—and quite thankfully—*Solo-Processing* is possible.

TAKING FLIGHT ON THE PATHWAY

Processing Techniques are intended to treat the *Spiritual Being* or *Alpha-Spirit*; the individual themselves. The *"command-lines"* are *directed to* the individual themselves—not some *mental machinery* of theirs, and not even a *Biofeedback* metering device.

Systematic Processing is applied by the *Alpha-Spirit*—who then *Self-directs* command of their "Mind-System" or "body" (*genetic-vehicle*), both of which are "constructs" that the *Alpha-Spirit* (*Self*, or the "I-AM" *Awareness unit*) operates, but neither of which is actually *Self*. *Fragmentation* causes *Humans* to falsely identify *Self as* the "*Mind*" or even a "*Body*."

Some *processes* can be treated quite lightly at first; others may require a bit of working at in order to get "*running*" well. It is important to set aside a period of time when you can be dedicated to your studies and *processing*. This period of time is referred to as a *"processing session."* When a *process* does start *running* well, it is important to be able to complete it to a satisfactory *"end-point."*

Processing allows us to be able to *actually* "look" at *things* and even determine the *considerations* we have made—or attitudes we have decided—about *Reality* as a result of those experiences.

It doesn't do us much good to simply "glance"—or to *restimulate* something uncomfortable and then quickly *withdraw* from it once again, leaving more of our *attention* yet again behind and held fixedly on it.

Generally speaking, a *Seeker* continues to *run* a *process* so long as something is "happening"—which is to say, the *process* is still producing a change. Usually this is evident by the type of "answers" that a *command-line* prompts a *Seeker* to originate from the database of their own *Mind-System*.

Processing Command-Lines ("PCL") are not "magic words"; they do not "do" anything on their own. They systematically assist a *Seeker* to direct their own attention toward increasing *Awareness*.

A *Seeker* may also cease to generate new "data" from a *process* without reaching an "*ultimate*" realization as an "*end-point*." It is possible that additional "layers" (or even other "areas") require handling before anything "deeper" is accessible. If this is the case, end the *process*. But, if a *Seeker* is *withdrawing* from something uncomfortable that was incited or stirred up, then a *process* is *run* until they feel "good" about it.

One of the benefits to *Flying-Solo* on the *Pathway* is that the *processing* is entirely *Self-determined*. This naturally provides a

17

certain built-in "safety" for a practitioner. Anything you *restimulate* by *Self-determinism* is *your thing*. It is not triggered or incited by some external *"other-determined"* influences (or other "source-points") that make you an *effect*. It can be more easily handled in *processing*—or you can simply let things "cool down" and come back to it again in another *session*.

While it may seem "mysterious" to beginners, a *Seeker* gets a sense for knowing how long to *run* a *process* only with practice. Once you have spent some time actually applying material from *"The Pathway to Ascension" Professional Course*, there are many aspects of it that become "second nature" because they are, in fact, a part of our true original native nature. All we have done in *Systemology* is *"reverse engineer"* the routes of *creation* and *consideration* that are already *our own*.

SYSTEMOLOGY LEVEL-8

We are publishing *"upper-level"* *Systemology* in 2024 for the very first time. Its effective application is dependent on a *Seeker* having already reached a stable point of *"Beta-Defragmentation."* This requires proper use of materials for *processing-levels 0 to 6*—as given in the *"Pathway to Ascension"* Professional Course (available in two volumes, or sixteen individual booklets).

Additionally, this current *Systemology Level-8* work is a direct continuation of *Level-7*, which *must* be completed before continuing. The *Systemology Level-7* manuals—*"The Secret of Universes," "Games, Goals & Purposes," "The Jewel of Knowledge"* and (to a lesser extent) *"Implanted Universes"*—should be treated as a single *"unit"* of work *prior* to approaching *Level-8*. These manuals are available individually, or as collected in *Volume One* of the *"Keys to the Kingdom"* *Advanced Training (A.T.) Course*.

After uncovering *"The Jewel"* and discovering the "secret" of *Universes*, a *"Seeker"* has *found* the "hidden gem" of the *Pathway* at *Level-7*, and is no longer a *"Seeker."* Of course, things are not always what we expect—and *"all that glitters is not gold."* Yet, still, it is *"The Jewel of Knowledge"* (*Parts #1-5*) and the *Entry-Point Heaven Incident*, *&tc.*, that represents the "ceiling" of *this Universe* and even what is behind it, beneath it, or embedded into its structure. It was what a *"Seeker"* had been *drawn* to in their *search*, but was never meant to find by any other method or avenue, except *systematically*.

Systemology Level-8 is the first official *"Wizard Level"* of the *Systemology Society*. As stated in *A.T. Manual #4*: while "formal" *Advanced Training* may end with manuals representing *Systemology Level-8* (and completing the "*Keys to the Kingdom*" series), this will also open up, what is referred to by the *Mardukite Academy* as, the "*Infinity Grade.*" [For instructional purposes, we tend to still refer to a practitioner as a "*Seeker*" in the *upper-level* manuals.]

There is no finite end-point to the "*Infinity Grade*" because its ultimate goal is the "*increase of spiritual perception,*" which is, in essence, *unlimited.* This means that plenty of room remains for future researchers to contribute; but only after first completing their *Advanced Training* regarding the parts of our "*Map*" that are *already* researched, well-plotted, effective in application, and thus published.

A *Seeker* could complete *A.T. Manual #3*, and then move on directly to *Level-8* with *A.T. Manual #5* ("*Entities & Fragments*"). If, however, a *Seeker* doesn't have enough "*reality*" on that *Level-8* material—as in, it doesn't seem *"real"* enough to them—then some time studying *A.T. Manual #4* (*"Implanted Universes"*) may be of benefit. The covert purpose of introducing *"Implant Platforms #1-18"* *(AT#3)* and the *"IPU Platforms"* *(AT#4)* at *Level-7*, is really to make *"Entities & Fragments"* *(AT#5)* more accessible.

To apply *upper-level Systemology*, an *advanced Seeker* must follow the prescribed outline of instruction that is now available for the first time to the public as the *"Keys to the Kingdom"* series.

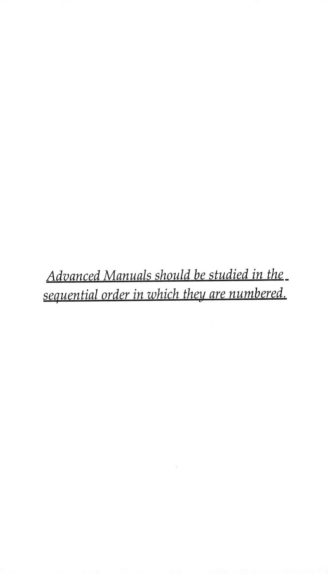

Advanced Manuals should be studied in the sequential order in which they are numbered.

Keep these prerequisite materials accessible:
PC Lesson-9, "Confronting The Past"
PC Lesson-10, "Lifting The Veils"
PC Lesson-11, "Spiritual Implants"
PC Lesson-12, "Games & Universes"
PC Lesson-13, "Spiritual Energy"
PC Lesson-14, "Spiritual Machinery"
AT Manual #1, "The Secret of Universes"
AT Manual #2, "Games, Goals & Purposes"
AT Manual #3, "The Jewel of Knowledge"
AT Manual #4, "Implanted Universes"

A.T. MANUAL #5
ENTITIES &
FRAGMENTS

LEVEL-8: "THE WIZARD GRADE"

Welcome to *Systemology Level-8*.

In this manual, we begin handling the *upper-level "Wizard Grade"* work of *defragmenting "spiritual entities and identity-fragments."* We have a very specific and *systematic* way of approaching this subject. A *Seeker* is advised not to mix or blend *other* beliefs and practices (for these topics) during this *training* and *processing*.

After a true successful completion of *"The Jewel; Parts #1-5" (AT#3)*, a *Seeker* no longer applies *processing-levels 0 to 4* to *"defragment"* their *own* case. [If more than a month has passed since completing the *Level-7 Stabilization Exercises (AT#3)*, it may be beneficial for a *Seeker* to repeat these before *Level-8*.]

A *Seeker* does not use *A.T. Levels* to handle *fragmentation* that should have been treated earlier on *The Pathway*. Any specific *"imprinted"* area of concern—or where *attention* is *"fixed"* in this lifetime—that *can* be handled with *processing-levels 0 to 6*, must be treated prior to *Advanced Training*—but most certainly before applying (or even studying) *Systemology Level-8*.

Assuming that all prerequisite *defragmentation* work is completed through *Level-7 (AT#3)*, a *Level-8 "Wizard"* should not be *running "imprint-chains"* on *themselves*. If it hasn't been completed, then the *Seeker* should have at least reached an *end-realization* with *"The Jewel,"* that they, themselves, are the ones keeping these *"chains"* in persistence, and holding them in place with *"attention units"* compulsively *"fixed"* outside their *actual Awareness* (or *Knowingness*).

At this point, simply *"Spotting"* areas of former *Not-Knowingness* is often enough to *defragment* them with *high-power attent-*

ion-Awareness. Understand that: *knowingly "Imagining"* (*creating* and *destroying*) *"mental imagery"* of the *past* for inspection, at will, is quite different than persistent *"imprinted imagery"* from those points on the *Backtrack* where parts of our *attention-Awareness* have been compulsively *"fixed"* or *"stuck."*

If a *Level-8 "Wizard"* still tries to *run "imprint-chains"* on themselves—even though a *Level-8* doesn't have any more of these *"fragmented chains"*—the *Wizard* will still *"find"* imprinting-chains to *process*. But this time, the *"imagery"* or *"content"* doesn't necessarily even make sense, because it is generally supplied by *other entities* (in close proximity to us); it is, in essence, *someone else's imprinting* that is being *"pulled-in"* as our own. As a *Seeker* knows—from studying *"source-points," "cause,"* and *"creation"*—we cannot effectively *defragment* something *"As-It-Is,"* when it is *"mis-owned"* or *"misidentified."*

While there are some *"spiritual perception"* exercises from *processing-levels 0 to 4* that may still be applied to *Self*, those that pertain specifically to *"imprinting"* —or *"confronting-the-past"* by *"incident-chains"* — should no longer be applied at *Level-8*. The *exception* here is: unless they are *directed to an entity other than Self* (and even then, they are often only *run* for *Circuit-1*).

By *"defragmenting spiritual entities...,"* we mean very literally: a *Level-8 "Wizard"* (acting as *Co-Pilot*), directing *defragmentation processing* to other *entities (as Seekers)* in order to *release them*. In this wise, our philosophy differs from other approaches. At *Level-8*, the directive is: *freeing entities from ourselves*, rather than *freeing ourselves from them*. This is to say: *releasing them* from their *entrapped fragmented* state, rather than the idea of *ridding* ourselves of them.

The handling of *spiritual entities and frag-*

ments is a critical part of the *"Wizard"* work. While a *Seeker* may have *defragmented* their own case to a point of *Self-Honesty*, they are still operating (on *Earth* and in the *Human Condition*) in close proximity to heavily *fragmented low-Awareness entities, identity-fragments* and other *"spiritual machinery."* Hence, this is where we place our emphasis at *Systemology Level-8*.

Study all material in *A.T. Manual #5* (*"Entities & Fragments"*) several times before applying any of its procedures. There are several techniques and methods provided in the text. A *Seeker* should be familiar with *all* of them before proceeding with any application. They are each *systematically* applied for a specific purpose, or in a specific sequence, to handle any layers of *spiritual "Alpha" fragmentation* that remain from previous *processing-levels.*

Having now introduced this new *gradient*

level of work, let us take up this subject from the top...

SPIRITUAL FRAGMENTATION

As an *Alpha-Spirit*, you are capable of *being* in many places at once. The *Alpha-Spirit* is able to operate *from* many places at once—because, of course, our *actual Beingness* is not actually "located" anywhere. It can, however, *consider* that "*parts*" or "*units*" of its *attention* (or *Awareness*) *are* located somewhere in sometime. Earlier *processing-levels* included exercises to aid in *unfolding* such *realizations*.

By "*located*," we mean systematically: wherever an individual places their *attention*, wherever they *perceive* from, wherever *intention* is *projected*, whatever *point-of-view* they are *operating* from, is where an individual is *located*. Maintaining multiple located viewpoints simultaneously is something that an *Alpha-Spirit* can do *knowingly—at will*. This natural ability—innate to all *Alpha-Spirits*—has simply been *fragmented* to one's own detriment.

Fragmentation occurs when we allow our *attention* to get *entrapped* in specific "*locations*"—then afterward burying our *knowingness* of it; intentionally "*Not-Knowing*" it, instead of either *knowingly operating from* it, or properly *withdrawing attention-units from* it. By this point on the *Pathway*, a *Seeker* should be increasingly *aware* that there are "hidden" or "compartmented" *fragments* of *Self* that continue to *unknowingly operate* (on *automatic*).

We are actually putting out "bits" of ourselves, our *thoughts* and *attention*—our *Awareness*, so to speak—all the time. We "*project*" this into the *Physical Universe* in order to perceive *impressions*, which allow us to *create* (or *duplicate*) appropriate im-

33

agery and sensation for our own experience. This is how we *perceive* "walls" and *interact* "or communicate" with others that share in the *Game* of this *Universe*. We *create* and *dissipate* these "bits" of *Awareness* (or "ZU") at will, simply by focusing *intention* and *attention*.

We *descended* as *spiritual beings*—through many *Universes*—and the decline of our *actualized Awareness* is proportional to the amount of *spiritual fragmentation* that has occurred. As a *spiritual being* "decays," they begin to "abandon" things, rather than "dissolving" them; this leaves many "bits" of themselves behind—"*unconscious*" but persistently running on *automatic*.

Earlier *processing-levels* will have allowed a *Seeker* to regain control over some of these "*split-pieces*." A littl was regained, for example, when we have extended our *Awareness* on the *Backtrack* and "*spotted*" or "*confronted*" something that we had formerly left some part of our *attention* on. Another critical area, *"spiritual machinery,"* is introduced in *PC Lesson-14*; but we only scraped the surface when treating such *"fragments."*

LOCATIONAL PROCEDURE

This *process* was developed specifically for *"split-fragments"*—but it also applies to other *entities*, which is why we introduce it first. Since it applies to both *"fragments"* and *"entities,"* a *Seeker* doesn't have to be too concerned whether they are treating a *"split-off"* piece of themselves or *"something else."*

A *"split-off"* piece of an individual is not a *"separate being"* (or actual *"entity"*), but it can *"act"* as though it is. It is really a *"part"* of themselves—usually sent off somewhere, hidden, and otherwise kept *operating unknowingly*. These *"fragments"* can be *aware*, in the sense that they *perceive*, *record*, and *react* to what is happening (based on *computations*)—but they are not *aware* of their own "*thinkingness*."

One of the challenges originally faced with this work concerns the fact that we, as individual *Alpha-Spirits*, have been *split-off* and *divided* many times—been *spiritually fragmented* over and over again. *Systematically* speaking: a *Seeker* cannot usually reclaim a "piece" of themselves directly, *if* both "*it*" and "*you*" have been *fragmented* further (subsequent to the original point of *division*). [The figure here is for illustrative purposes only.]

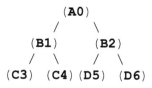

In this example: if (C3) is the *conscious viewpoint* (or *Seeker*), and it locates the presence of (D6) and tries to "rejoin" that part directly (using other procedures), the *Seeker* will be unsuccessful (and potentially feel "ill"). This is because such "bypasses" *missing* "*fragments*" that are essentially "*in between.*" The "*Locational Procedure*" resolves this issue for *our own* "*spiritual fragments*" (on which other techniques are unworkable). The *in-session procedure* is rather simple:

If you *get a sense of* (or *spot*) something that might be a *split-off* part of yourself, an *isolated* (*compartmented*) *fragment* of something (or someone), or an *entity* (or some *identity-fragment*) that is blocked from (or blocking) your *Awareness*—then you *direct to* "*it*" the *processing command-line* (PCL):

"*Point To The Being That You Divided From.*"

This is an important technique for a *Seeker* to "fall back on"—as a remedy or "*repair action*"—if any difficulties arise when applying other material from this manual. [It is also effective on *fragments* of *others* that are "stuck" on *us*; so you don't have to know the exact nature of *what* you are applying it to.]

The *"pointing"* is really a *direction* of *attention*—or *"spotting"* with *Awareness*. It is a "mental action" and is not limited to *three-dimensions* or a *Physical Universe* *"direction."* It is not even *"pointing"* toward (or *"spotting"*) where the *"other being"* is *now*; rather it focuses *attention* on the original *"direction"* where the *"split"* occurred. [If some remnant seems to remain thereafter, a *Seeker* may then apply the *"Identity Procedure"* directly to it (as given later).]

The PCL (above) is also beneficial for handling *entities* (*self-aware spiritual beings* or *Alpha-Spirits*), which includes the *Seeker* themselves. One will notice (if the PCL is applied directly to *Self*) that *you* do not "dissolve" or "rejoin" someone else. A separate individual *entity* (*Alpha-Spirit*) gets a better sense of *Self*, or who they are. However, when treating a *fragment*, it dissolves the separation. A *fragment* has no reason to remain separate, unlike the case of an actual individual *Alpha-Spirit*.

"*Split-off pieces*" and "*spiritual fragments*" (of ourselves or others) are different from individual *entities*. An *Alpha-Spirit* can also "*divide*" into two completely separate *entities*. In other words, both parts will have the complete prior *Backtrack* of the other; neither is senior. There is no loss of *spiritual ability*; both are identical—and both have identical memory of *being* the *original* that *divided*. Such results in two completely separate individual evolving spiritual beings that will never "rejoin" because each is now a full *Alpha-Spirit*.

In *Meta-Systemology*, it is theorized that approximately only *10,000* individual *Alpha-Spirits* separated from the "*Infinity-of-Nothingness*" at one time and went through the original *Jewel* incident into this particular "*womb of existence*" (prior to *Home Universe*). [Ref: *AT#1 & 3*.] These individuals eventually *divided* many times, leading to the *trillions* that now inhabit *this Physical Universe*.

True individual *Alpha-Spirits* do not "rejoin"—because such would reduce the *infinitude of creation* that is balancing the *Infinity-of-Nothingness*. "Fragments" on the other hand, whether your own or someone else's, are not separate units of "*Self-Awareness*." These *fragments can* "rejoin"—and usually with great benefit, by restoring *Awareness* to areas that the *Alpha-Spirit* was handling *unknowingly* (and can now treat *knowingly*).

A *Seeker* should *not* make the mistake of thinking that *they* (*themselves*) are a subordinate piece of some kind of bigger "*Uber-Alpha*" or "*over-soul*." There *are* "*upper-level compartments of ourselves*" that *operate unknowingly*, or that we are typically blocked from being *aware* of directly; but that is not a separate *entity*—it is the *"higher parts"* of our *Self*, which we "unfold" an increasing conscious *Awareness* of, as we *Ascend*.

There is also some *"splitting"* (of *Awareness*) that occurs naturally. For example: you put "bits" of yourself on people and places (*terminals*)—using *intention* and *attention*—that you want to keep track of, or influence. Since these are not *"enforced"* by anyone, they can simply be brought under conscious control. There's nothing that inhibits you from dissolving (or controlling) these "pieces" except your own worries over being able to put them back, or losing track of things.

A *Seeker* can actually master consciously dissolving these *"splits"* and putting them back out. All that is necessary is to practice *"projecting"* and *"dissolving"* these *"split-pieces"* at will. Once a *Seeker* has certainty on this ability, they will be able to let go of the ones that aren't wanted. Part of their *compulsive persist-*

ence is the lack of *certainty* on this skill—because there is a natural tendency to form these "connections" to others people (and *terminals*) in order to stay in the *Game* of *this Physical Universe*.

The *"splitting"* of *attention*—or our *projecting "pieces"*—is not the actual *fragmentation*. The *fragmentation* occurs when a *"split"* takes place without one's conscious control (or *Awareness*), and also when one loses control and *Awareness* over the *pieces* that have already *split*. This is what takes place under the heavy spiritual impact of *Implanting*.

FRAGMENTS & BONDED-ENTITIES

When we refer to *"entities"* in *Systemology*, we usually mean other individual disembodied *Alpha-Spirits* (without ownership and control of their own *"Human Body"*). We introduce this subject at *Level-*

8, after a *Seeker* has a handle on their own case from previous levels. *Entities* (and *fragments, &tc.*) are not a primary source of *fragmentation*; at best, they might "block" *Awareness*, or amplify our own *fragmentation*.

The *entities* we are most concerned with at this point are those which are adhesively attached to *you* or your *Human Body*. These *Bonded-Entities* has been with the *Alpha-Spirit* for a long time. They generally remain *stuck* in a *low-Awareness level* that is tied to *misemotional states* such as: anger, resentment, anxiety, terror/fear, depression, and hopelessness. They seem to be most "active" when an individual is also operating at those levels, which tends to contribute to such states persisting.

But understand that if you're "angry" (for example), it is *your* "anger"—it does not stem from an *entity* or some kind of *demon*. However, just as a living person might "fan the flames" to encourage a greater *dramatization* of your anger, so too with *entities*, or even *fragments* of yourself. While these *fragments* mainly operate on *automatic*, they still respond to what you are "feeling" and other "reactivity." As a *Seeker* increases their *actualized Awareness*, they can operate greater control over these "*mechanisms*" and other areas.

[If at any point, "something" gets restimulated or stirred up by reading the descriptions and instructions in this manual, apply the *Locational Procedure* to "*it*."]

A *Seeker* will recall a common theme of "*being divided*" in the *Implant Penalty Universes* (IPU) described in *A.T. Manual #4*. Whether this *actually* occurred to the *Alpha-Spirit* during those *incidents*, or were only *represented* in one's virtual/holographic experience of them, is still under research. But, in either case: the concepts present in the IPU all become reoccurring themes for *actual* events in later (more recent) *Universes.*

There are many ways in which a division or *"split"* might occur. When one is "divided against themselves," they make an individual be in two places, and then might *Implant* each location with different *goals* that are "antagonistic" to each other. This will cause each *viewpoint* to essentially *fight against* the other one—continuously applying *counter-efforts* against each other. A *"splitting"* could also take place if an individual were impacted heavily with *force.*

There have been large-scale mass-*Implanting Incidents* that forced an individual to put *"pieces"* of themselves onto *others*, in order to *control* them and *keep* them *"human."* Similarly, there have been "advanced" societies that employed *"Police Implants"* —which caused you to make *"split-pieces"* into *"Control Entities"* that

45

were placed on "criminals." [Some of these societies made all citizens do this regularly as part of their civic duty or taxation.]

There is information on the *Backtrack* about specialized "collectives." In their advanced military campaigns, officers would put *"split-off pieces"* as *"Control Entities"* onto their subordinates—all the way down the chain-of-command—so that an *"invasion force"* could operate as a single "unit" under the command of a single *Alpha-Spirit* (at the top).

In the *"wizarding"* societies of the *Magic Universe*, "entities" were often the high-value *"coin"* or *currency*. They were often used as servants or laborers—or even entrapped in *"objects"* to make "magical devices." One of the reasons the *Human Condition* is susceptible to *"Bonded-Entities"* is because of the accumulated *postulates* and *considerations* regarding the "*acquiring*" of *entities* for some kind of use.

And while we have introduced the subject of "*spiritual machinery*" in earlier *processing-levels* (see *PC-14*), the subject will be treated more thoroughly in this manual. But briefly stated: we have, at times, intentionally put out *pieces* to set up "*machinery*" (in various *non-physical directions*) in order to project the *reality* we *perceive* for ourselves. This too, eventually became fragmented and out of our conscious control as a result of the heavy impacts from certain *Implanting-Incidents*.

In *processing-levels 0 to 6*, the "*Seeker*" themselves is the main focus or target of *processing-sessions*. Of course, on the *Pathway* toward *Ascension*, a *Seeker* is actually treating a "composite case" of:

Self + Human Body + Bonded-Entitites

The fundamental *processing-levels* ensure that an individual—the *Seeker*—ceases in compulsively "mucking up" things for themselves. In this wise, a clear view is available for handling everything that is apart from us; that keeps us entrapped in *this Physical Universe, the Human Condition,* and *on Earth.*

Once a strong foundation is in place—a *Seeker* has reached stable *Beta-Defragmentation* with *processing-levels 0 to 6*—and the more significant *turbulent charge* is *defragmented* from the *Implanting* described in *Level-7,* no further *imprinting* must be *processed-out* on the individual's *own case.*

Using those procedures *on Self,* from *Level-8* onward will have a tendency to "pull-in" the *imprinting* and *fragmentation* of other *entities* that hang suspended in "close proximity" to us—such as *Bonded-Entities.* There are ways of applying earlier *processes* directly *to entities* in order to *intentionally* make these *entities* accessible for proper handling; but a *Seeker* must *knowingly* be doing so to be successful. Otherwise, the risks associated with this phenomenon is a *misidentification* of *source/cause*—which results in persistence of the *fragmentation* that is not handled *As-It-Is*.

It is possible, even after *processing-levels 0 to 7*, that a *Seeker* still experiences some *fixation* on specific "*reoccurring items*" or *turbulently charged* "*areas*" that did not seem to fully "*release*" or *defragment*. Assuming previous *levels* were fully completed, it is likely—at *Level-8*—that such *charge* persists due to the "*protest*" (*restimulation*) of a *Bonded-Entity* or B.E. We want to, however, make certain that we are not treating something *as someone else's*, which is really *our own* (and the other way around).

At this high-level of operation, a "*Wizard's*" primary *processing-action* is now "*Spotting As-It-Is; and Defragmentation by Awareness.*" This requires the ability to

properly *recognize* a true *identification* of
"Source" and *"What Is,"* &tc., which a
Seeker will have strongly developed along
the *Pathway.* This is applied directly in
systematic processing with the *"Identification Procedure"* (given below)—which is
effective whether handling a *Bonded Entity,* a *split-fragment (spiritual machinery),*
or even the *genetic-vehicle (Body)* that is
also an *entity.*

THE IDENTIFICATION PROCEDURE

This technique is incredibly basic, though
its actual application and background requires additional explanation. Its origins
are as old as there have been *Wizards* and
Priests attempting to exercise control over
other *entities.*

Once you *locate (get a sense of, &tc.)* a *being, entity,* or *fragment,* you *direct to "it"*

the following *process*—which includes
two *steps* (or PCL):

A. *"What Are You?"*

B. *"Who Are You?"*

Use of this technique requires knowing
the difference between something being
"in-phase" versus *"out-of-phase."* There is
some mention of *personality-phases* in past
Systemology literature, but what we really
mean is *Identity-phases* or *Identity-phasing*.

By *"phase,"* we mean: *being* something
other than *who* and *what* you are (an *Alpha-Spirit*), but *mistakenly* operating from
that *viewpoint* or *point-of-view* (POV) as
though it is your *actual Identity* (*compulsively* and/or *unknowingly*). This is what
people mean by the phrase "lose themselves"—which is to say *"out-of-synch"*
with *Truth* or *Self-Honesty*. [Use of the
term *"phase"* comes from *electrical-wave
engineering*, but its application here is *systematically* accurate.]

Fundamentals of this procedure do not require a lot of technical complexity. The first step is understanding that you are in close proximity to other *entities* (*Alpha-Spirits*) that have not shared the full benefit of the same *processing* that has delivered *you* to this point on the *Pathway*. Therefore, the same type of personal *fragmentation* treated at *processing-levels 0 to 4*, which once held up a *Seeker*, could also be what is keeping an *entity* from "*releasing*"—but in this case, we would direct such *defragmentation processing* to the *entity*.

When we speak of *Identities* and *phases*, we are *systematically* referring to the "*conception and/or perception of one's own Beingness.*" *Bonded-Entities* can become *fixated* on any *Identity-phase*, just as any other *Alpha-Spirit* can. The *Identity-phase* that an *entity* may be in, is not restricted to "an individual person"; it is not restricted to a "*body*" or even traditional *terminals*. Of course, one's true and actual nature is *Self* —the *(Alpha)-Spirit*.

An *entity* may be *identifying (out-of-phase)* with anything: a role, a name, a significance, a word (or phrase), a group, a body part, or really any material object—from molecules to planets. It may also have been *Implanted* with a *goal*, which is to say a *"doingness"* that it *identifies* with even more than a *"Beingness"* —such as *"a goal to block (you),"* or of *"being a barrier,"* &tc.

In many ways, the *Identification Procedure* is a *"listing-process"* for an *entity.* You may need to get multiple answers for the *"What..?"* PCL until you can determine what they are currently *being.* It is important to *"acknowledge"* any of the answers/responses/impressions that are perceived/received (just as in *Traditional Piloting/Co-Piloting*). A familiarity with *Systemology Piloting* is necessary for *systematically processing entities.*

Initially, this procedure is best practiced by writing out the question on your worksheet, then listing out the answers —preferably using *GSR-Meter* "reads" as an *indicator* of the "most correct" answer.

Just as with *Co-Piloting* any other *Seeker*, it is important not to "*invalidate*" any response; but you can *process* an *entity toward* a *release-point* by getting it "*in phase.*" When using the procedure, whether you are freeing an individual *Alpha-Spirit*, or you are returning a *fragment* to its *source*, you are unburdening yourself from carrying the *fragmentation*, and increasing the *Awareness* of other *Alpha-Spirits* in the *Universe*.

Once they *recognize* that they are not the "*phase-item*," you direct the "*Who..?*" PCL with the intention that they will answer "*Me*" or "*I'm Me*" (from the perspective of the *entity*). This is meant to restore their *Awareness* that they are nothing else but simply themselves. The *entity* will often *release* after you *acknowledge* the correct answer—as if it finally *realizes*: "*Oh, I really am me!*"

If the answer you get is not "*Me,*" you still *acknowledge* the response, but you will probably have to repeat the PCL. It may also require some basic *two-way communication* with the *entity* in order to steer them toward the "*Me*"-type answer. For example:

"*What were you before that?*"

This shifts the *entity's attention* to an earlier point on their *Backtrack*. Effectiveness of the *Identification Procedure* is dependent on resolving misconceptions about *Identity* that the *entity* (*fragment, &tc.*) is fixated on.

BONDED-ENTITIES & FUSED-GROUPS

There are two main aspects of instruction for this subject that are alternated throughout this manual: a) the understanding of *Bonded-Entities* and *Fused-Groups* in order to recognize, locate, and contact them; b) the *systematic methods* by which these *entities* can be released by a "*Wizard-level*" practitioner. It may be the case at times that many *entities* are "showing up" for *defragmentation processing*; and a true "*Wizard*" must handle them orderly, civilly, respectfully, lovingly, firmly, ...*systematically.*

Presence of *Bonded-Entities* (or "B.E.") will block or inhibit the clarity and horsepower of our *spiritual perception* (*ZU-Vision, &tc.*)—yet most are not malevolent themselves, they are just sort of *low-Awareness beings* "in the way." It might be helpful to think of *"layers"* (or *sheets*) of interconnected 1-cm. (half-inch) *marbles* or *beads* that surround the *body* (like a tight skin-suit) and even penetrate it. These sheets, although mainly transparent and resembling the structure of modern *bubble-wrap*, "stack up" as *layers,* often extending out approximately three-feet from the *body.*

The *Seeker* should practice being able to *focus, concentrate,* and *concenter* (permeate from all directions), their own *"attention"* to a *spot* that is 1-centimeter (or half-inch) —the approximate area that an *entity* is perceived to relatively occupy as a *viewpoint-for-Awareness* in *Space.* A *Seeker* would have some practice in this area from the *"objective exercises"* found in former *processing-levels.* This is an important skill for *communicating with (processing)* a single specific *entity.*

A *Level-8* practitioner has a high-level of

Awareness, but still must limit *attention* to one *entity* at a time until its *release*.

In addition to individual B.E., there is another phenomenon that occurs, which we refer to as a *"Fused-Group."* These *groups* consist of multiple B.E. that are held (or *fused*) together by a shared traumatic, heavily fragmentary, experience—usually a heavy *Implanting-Incident*. By *processing-out* the *fusing incident*, a *Fused-Group* may be *dispersed, released* as a whole, or at least broken up into individual B.E. for *release*.

Fused-Groups "formation" and B.E. "adhesion" often results from heavy *impacts*—such as with at least one significant *Implanting-Incident* we know of that took place in *this Physical Universe*. When an *entity* (*Alpha-Spirit*) forcefully collides (*impacts*) with another *entity*, either (or both) may get so heavily *imprinted* with a *"mental image picture"* of the *impact* that it gets its *consideration-of-Beingness* "stuck" or "fused"—*out-of-phase*—to the *imprint*

58

and the other *entity* that shares the *imprint*.

While an *Alpha-Spirit (Seeker)* operates with a *Human Body*, it acts as a *filter* and *magnifier* for an individual's *perception* and experience of *reality*. True *spiritual perception* (*ZU-Vision* and other innate *Alpha abilities*) is far more accessible to an individual after clearing all *identifications* with *bodies* that are not *Self*. This includes handling B.E. (and *Fused-Groups*), because once they are fixated on their *identification* with the *Human Body*, they form an *encysted* solidity and *crystallized* "shell" or "aura" that acts to hold an individual (*Seeker*) *in* the *Human Condition*.

Some B.E. are intentionally *implanted* to be part of a *body* (a specific *body-part* or *spot* on a *body*)—which is *out-of-phase* with their *being* an *Alpha-Spirit* or *fragment*, &tc. Operating in this wise, most *entities* believe they are serving a specific purp-

ose, going so far as to think they are being helpful, or even necessary.

A B.E. (or *Fused-Group*) is not really *aware*
of their *presence* in *"present-time"* —their
attention/Awareness being very much *fixed*
on a *past incident*. In order to *release* an *entity*, it may be necessary to *process them* to
a point of *confronting that incident*. This is
accomplished *systematically* with the
*Level-8 "Incident-Running Procedure (for
Entities)"* given in the next section.

Due to the proximity of B.E. and *fragments*, there is a *"telepathic link"* by which
contact/communication is possible (for *processing*). This *link* is *knowingly* (*consciously*) accessible to a *Seeker/Wizard* at
Level-8, given the nature of study and
heightened *Awareness* already achieved
on the *Pathway*. This manual concerns *defragmenting* one's own *composite-case* (B.E.,
fragments, &tc.) and is not an esoteric
treatment concerning other types of
"spirits." The information and skill req-

uired to handle other kinds of *spiritualism* is generally acquired by a *Wizard* through the experience of handling what *is* accessible (and affecting their own case).

When a B.E. *defragments/releases* (usually upon "*acknowledgment*" of its proper *Identity*-answer, or some other *process*), the "*telepathic*" *link*, *cord*, or *bond*, also disperses. At the moment this takes place, a moment of "*exterior perception*" is sometimes *fed back* to the *Seeker*, but from the *viewpoint* of the *entity*. To be sure the *entity* "*happily blows off*," this occasional phenomenon should not be *invalidated*; but it should not be mistaken as one's own *ZU-Vision*. [Of course, increase of one's *spiritual perception* is a natural side-effect to *releasing* the *Alpha-fragmentation* that persists in blocking our *clarity*.]

During *processing-levels 0 to 7*, we don't generally handle much concerning *somatic-pings* or *bodily sensations* that "turn on" during *systematic sessions*. They might be *acknowledged*, but generally "turn off" when the *process* is *run* to a full *defragmentation-point*.

At *Level-8*—when treating *entities* and *incidents*—*sensations* and *pressures* felt from the *body* are more critical. If they occur while handling a *process*, record exactly *where* on the *body* they occur. Use this to data as a suggestion for where to focus your 1-cm. (half-inch) beam of *attention* during your next *process*. When applying *Level-8*, it is likely to be a B.E. coming "awake" or "active" and essentially saying: "*Here I am!*" [It is important not to just *pass-by* or *fly-by* such *indicators* at this *level*.]

When this does occur, it is important to *acknowledge* the *somatic-ping* and make a record (to return to later). You can even tell the *entity*: "*I hear you there, but you'll have to wait your turn.*" It is also important not to prematurely *end-off* the handling of a *current entity* until its *release*.

The standard practice is to check for any other *entities* at the same location you were just handling, to be sure it wasn't a *Fused-Group* or if another B.E. moved in to duplicate its position. Then, if the former *somatic-ping* persists (that occurred while working with the other), you can check for an *entity* at *that* location. It is good practice to work with different areas of the body each session, rather than checking over the same parts consecutively. Extend your *Awareness* or *perception* to areas from different sides or angles.

In addition to *somatic-pings* (*pressure, pain, sensations*), B.E. and *Fused-Groups* may communicate by relaying *emotion* (*feelings*), an *audible voice* (*perceived internally*), or some type of "*thought*" or "*imagery.*" *Contacting* (*communicating* with) B.E. for *processing* can also be accomplished directly with even the most faint of *perceived impressions*, if a *Seeker* is proficient with a *GSR-Meter/biofeedback device* (which is the preferred *systematic method* of handling this area/subject). If a *"Wizard"* can focus their *attention-Awareness* specifically on the *energetic-mass* of *one entity*, then that B.E. will *react/register "answers"* on a *Meter* (just like any *Seeker*).

Advisement: there could easily be *over 100 Fused-Groups* and individual *Bonded-Entities* adhesively fixed to a *Seeker*. If you find *zero*, or only a few, it is quite possible that you are not yet at a "level" to *confront Level-8* work. Make certain all your fundamentals (*processing-levels 0 to 6*) "check out" okay. If you are certain that your own handling of *"The Jewel (Parts #1-5)"* is properly *defragmented* (from *AT#3*), run *"Platforms #1-18"* (again) from that manual. Additional details regarding *"Platforms #1-18"* also appears in this manual.

Let's start with a basic exercise to increase your *spiritual perception* for *handling entities*.

1. *Close your eyes.*

2. *"Imagine"* (*create by visualization*) a B.E. as a sort of *"circle of energy"* or *"pressure."*

3. *Acknowledge it* (for being there).

4. *"Imagine/Intend"* for the B.E. to *release*— leaving and disappearing into the distance (as a result of your *recognizing* and *acknowledging* it).

Repeat this exercise many times, *"imagining/creating"* these in various locations: in precise *points* in the *body*, in precise *spots-in-space* around you, in the *walls*, *floor*, and *ceiling*, &tc. Continue until you feel good about this exercise and your certainty in doing it. Then run the *"Standard Procedure (for Entities)"* and see if there are any more accessible now.

A *Seeker* should be able to notice the slight difference between the "feel" (or "sense of") the *actual* B.E. versus those they have intentionally *imagined/created*.

There are times (at *Level-8*) where a *Seeker* will think they've *Spotted* (or *sensed*) a real one, when they're really *imagining/creating* it there. But that's okay.

If you *release* a few *"imagined"* ones from an area, it will be easier to handle the real ones anyways. They even sometimes *"copy the imagery"* of you *releasing* the *imagined* ones and will leave along with it. Once you have *certainty* with the *systematic processing* of *entities* — and have elevated your own *Actualized Awareness* — most types of *entities* and *fragments* can be *dispersed* by simply *"acknowledging"* them and *"defrag-by-Awareness"* (*As-It-Is*).

INCIDENT-RUNNING PROCEDURE
(*for bonded-entities, fused-groups*)

[A *Seeker* should review *"Confronting the Past"* (*PC-9*), *"Spiritual Implants"* (*PC-11*) and *"Games & Universes"* (*PC-12*). Keep these materials accessible—in addition to "Secret of Universes" (AT#1) and "The Jewel of Knowledge" (AT#3)—when applying the "Incident-Running Procedure (for Entities)."]

Unlike when a Seeker has run incidents and incident-chains for previous levels—such as in "Confronting the Past" (PC-9)—we only use Implanting-Incidents for which we have significant data, when handling entities. This means that we do not have to find out "what happened" from each entity in order to defragment them.

When applying processing to entities: we don't need to go through every detail of an incident, or implant-item of a Platform; simply get the entity to spot the main highlights. In this wise, we can very pointedly direct a PCL to an entity to "Go To.." or "Move To.." such-and-such part of an incident sequence.

To be effective, the *Seeker/Wizard* must maintain control of the *session*, just like a *Pilot*—directing PCL to B.E. in order to "guide" their *attention* through the *sequence* of the *incident*; directing them to *spot* various points from a "*sequence outline*" that is already known to the *Seeker/Wizard*. As you gain experience with handling this procedure, you'll have greater certainty on your ability to *telepathically* "blanket" and "push" an *entity* through the *incident* they are "stuck" in. [This serves to *release* them so they can *leave/blow-off*.]

When starting *Level-8*, there are two primary *Implanting-Incidents* that a *Seeker* first applies this procedure to. A *Seeker* has actually been studying the components of these in previous *processing-levels*.

— *The Heaven Incident* (at the start of our *track* in *this Universe*);

and

68

— *The Hellfire Incident* (which occurred 66 or 75 *million years ago*).

HEAVEN & HELLFIRE

The *"Hellfire Incident"* used for this *"Incident-Running Procedure"* does not need to be *processed* by a *Seeker* *"on Self."* Its appearance here is specifically for handling *Earth-bound entities* (B.E. and *Fused-Groups*) that are commonly affected by this particular *Implanting-Incident*. It assists in "breaking up" (or *dispersing*) *Fused-Groups* into individual B.E., freeing them up for additional individualized *processing* (through the *"Heaven Incident"*).

Applying the *"Hellfire Incident"* only treats a certain *layer* or segment of *entities* that were actually affected (or *fused*) by this *incident,* or are still "stuck" on it; but we apply this as a basic method because of the amount of gain that is achieved with it. It is not the only mass (widespread) *Implanting-Incident* that this general procedure applies to. [The *"Hellfire Incident"* is a specialized application that does not appear in the basic instructions for *"Standard Procedure: Entities"* (given in the next section).]

The *"Heaven Incident"* is the only *incident* that is *common to all entities* (*Alpha-Spirits*) that have experienced *Entry-Into-This-Universe*; but *only* an *individual* B.E. can be *released* by using it for this procedure. Therefore, the *"Hellfire Incident"* is *processed first*, in order to break up *"groups"* that were *fused* by that *incident* (before *running* individual *entities* through the *"Heaven Incident"*).

When the *"Hellfire Incident"* is applied to *handling entities*: you start with *"1. The Explosion,"* and *never* push the B.E. (or *Fused-Group*) beyond *"2B. Platforms #1-18"* in the *sequence outline*. To go further requires having full data on the *"36-Day Implant"* (that uses IPU symbols). There is not enough *data* to do so and still be in full control of the *session*. And it is not necessary for this procedure. If the B.E. hasn't *released* by that point, then you may need to *run* the *incident* a second time (starting with *The Explosion*). But, that may be unnecessary, because this much of the *incident sequence* is usually sufficient enough to disperse a *Fused-Group*—in which case, if *entities* remain, you can then take each *individual* B.E. through the *"Heaven Incident"* (and/or apply *"Standard Procedure"*).

Usually only the *"1. Heaven Implant"* section of the *"Heaven Incident"* is necessary for this procedure; and even a vague approximation of its events is effective. One of the issues with running *"The Jewel, Parts #1-5"* is that the same *Implant-Pattern* was later (more recently) repeated in the *"Hellfire Incident"* sequence. If a *Seeker/Wizard* finds they *do* need to direct an *entity* to *"Spot"* (or *"Go To.."*) specific parts of *The Jewel Implant* in order to *release* them, it is important to make sure that the *Pattern* is being treated for the right *incident*.

There is additional data for the *Hellfire Incident*, much of which is *speculative* at this juncture of our research. Since the data for the basic *"sequence outline"* is correct (effective), we haven't concerned ourselves with the other details that may be accessible. Whether or not the *incident* took place on *Earth*, or was all an elaborate *"projection,"* does not alter its demonstrable workability and effectiveness in breaking through the *Fused-Groups* of B.E. that are "stuck" on whatever this *Implanting-Incident* happens to really be. In *Systemology*, we are more concerned with *results*, than *dogma*—so we include the *incident* for the gains it provides.

What we do know is that the *atomic blasts*, *meteors* and *volcanism* indicated by the *Hellfire Incident* is a direct reference to what some refer to as *"The Great Dying"* —a cataclysmic period of synchronous events that *did* take place on *Earth*. Although some geologists and physicists date this event at approximately *66 million years ago,* the elevated *radiation* levels of the *incident* have caused the *carbon-dating* to be skewed on this one. When using *GSR-Metering,* the *incident* may be *"located and dated"* (as in it *"registers"*) at *75 million years ago.*

The *Hellfire Incident* was an intentionally planned event. It occurred in order to establish *Earth* as a *"prison planet"* for this *galaxy*—and also program the basic *"Human Condition"* for the *Alpha-Spirits* entrapped here. The *Earth* was actually a beautiful planet inhabited by diverse lifeforms; but like everything else in *this Universe,* it became *fragmented*—now *repurposed* to serve as a dumping ground for *entities* that were otherwise too numerous, or too free, to be adequately con-

{ <u>HEAVEN INCIDENT</u> }

0. ENTRY-INTO-UNIVERSE

1. HEAVEN IMPLANT
   (See PC-12 & AT#1)

   A.) Loud Sharp Snapping Crackles

   B.) Waves Of Light

   C.) Theater & Stage

   D.) Angel On Chariot Enters

   E.) Trumpet Blasts

   F.) Thundering Crackles and Snaps

   G.) Angel On Chariot Exits

   H.) "Goals-Sequencing" Pageant/Skit

   I.) Waves of Darkness

2. THE JEWEL (PARTS #1-5)
   (See AT#3 for details)

{ <u>HELLFIRE INCIDENT</u> }

0. CAPTURE/TRANSPORT
   (if Alpha-Spirit is not already on Earth)

1. EXPLOSION

   A.) Atomic, Volcanic, Meteor, *&tc.*
       (specific events and locations)

   B.) Terrible Winds

   C.) Alpha-Spirit Carried Into Sky

   D.) Electronic Field/Screen Rises In Sky

   E.) Alpha-Spirit Stuck To Screen

   F.) Pulled Down For Mass-Implanting

2. HELLFIRE IMPLANT

   A.) Jewel, Parts #1-5 *(for this incident)*
       Establishes false "Start-of-Time"

   B.) Platforms #1-18 Series *(see AT#3)*
       Programming of "Human Condition"

   C.) Arrival Of "The Pilot"

   D.) 36-Days Of IPU-Restimulation
       Holographic moving pictures (like film)
       (lacking data here; see AT#4)

3. ASSEMBLY CENTERS
   (may belong above as "1G")

   A.) Fusion Of Entities Into Groups
       (at specific locations)

trolled (by whatever society did the *implanting*).

More advanced societies in *this Universe* have something akin to "Implant Dealers." The *Implants* that appear in the *Hellfire Incident* are not original to that *incident*; but they were collected, chained together, and were effectively impactful. "*The Jewel (Parts #1-5)*" are repeated from the *Heaven Incident*, to install a false sense of the *Hellfire Incident* being the "*start of time.*" The "*#1-18 Series*" was primarily kept on file since the *Magic Universe* era (and even prior). Restimulation of the *Implanted Penalty-Universes* extends back several *Universes*. It is only important to *run through* the "items" on the *sequence outline*; you do not have to *run* all command-lines of all *Platforms* on each *entity* when applying this "*Incident-Running Procedure.*"

HELLFIRE INCIDENT
(ADDITIONAL DATA)

This section is included to increase a *Seeker's reality* on, and ability to effectively handle, the *Hellfire Incident-Running Procedure*. Our research phase demonstrated that it is an area—or point on this *Advanced Training* course—that some *Seeker's* seemed to get "stuck" on, which prevented continuing their studies/progress.

Although there are many *Implanting-Incidents* on the *Backtrack*, this one is included in this manual because it is "*spiritual contamination*" (or *fragmentation*) that is "common to all" *Earthlings*. While this seems like it should make our *Standard Procedures* more effective, many of the B.E. from this *incident* are initially found in an incredibly *low-Awareness state*, and often need a lot of assistance (*Beingness* or *livingness* granted to them by the "*Wizard*") in order to achieve their *release*.

In the past, "Mystics" often used various *tools* and *spiritual-aids* to accomplish their *"divination"* and *"necromancy."* Today, we have the benefit of using *Biofeedback-Devices* that allow us to approach these same areas far more *systematically.*

B.E. are located by *"Meter-read,"* checking off from the following list (in the order given): the location of a *current somatic-ping* (*pressure, itching, tingling, &tc.*); the location of a *between-session* discomfort; the location of a *Fused-Group* (from a previous *session* that is not fully handled); and general "scanning" or "looking around" the *body.*

Some B.E. require a greater *reality* on the *incident* they are "stuck" in before they are able to *confront* it *"As-It-Is."* This means, what we generally refer to as, *"dating and locating."* Remember that the *Hellfire Incident* is the kind of event that an individual might even *want* to *forget.*

So, the first part of *"incident-running"* might require more than the *processing-command* to just *"Go to...{start of incident}."*

We can easily determine the date as *"75 Million Years Ago."* [This may be indicated to the B.E./*Fused-Group*.] *"Locating"* the incident on the *Backtrack* as a *"date"* (in *Time*) does not always provide enough *reality* for the B.E. to properly *confront* it. Therefore, a *Seeker* may also need to *"locate"* the *incident "in Space"* —which means determining a literal/physical *geographic location*.

In the past, *"Mystics"* often used *"maps"* combined with such things as *"pendulums"* and *"dowsing-rods"* to accomplish these same *spiritual tasks*. Today's *"Wizard"* benefits strongly from using *"Biofeedback-Technology."*

To be in *contact* with an *entity*, a *"Wizard"* focuses high-level *attention* on the *entity*—

realizing "It-Is" there, *acknowledging* its *existence, &tc*. This grants a higher-level of *Beingness* or *livingness* to the *entity*—and between the two *beings*, there is a heightened "*combined-Awareness*" present for the *session*.

The *attention* and *proximity/affinity* (*telepathic link*) allow the *entity* to "*register*" on a *GSR-Meter*, even though it is the *Seeker/ Wizard* (having first *defragmented* the bulk of their own case) that is physically using the *Biofeedback-Device*. This idea might underlie any assumed effectiveness of such *spiritual-aids* as the "*ouija board*"— but again, we now have far more effective *systematic* means available to us today.

Therefore, with your *attention* on the *entity*, and a *combined-Awareness* on the *incident*: you can use a *GSR-Meter* "*sensor*" (in one hand), and your finger or pointer (with the other hand), and *scan* over a "map" of the *Earth* to find "*Meter-reads*" on actual *locations*. [This applies to more than just *running* the *Hellfire Incident*.]

Note that the continental arrangement of *Earth* was far different *75 million years ago* than it is today. You can "print out" (or otherwise obtain) *geologic estimations* of how the *Earth* appeared at that time, or you can use a modern-day *map*.

Our interest—when specifically handling the *Hellfire Incident*—is the location of the *"explosion site."* For this particular *incident*, it does not have to be exact; the *locations* can be approximated. We also aren't too concerned with whether the nature of that particular *explosion* was *"atomic/nuclear,"* *"meteoric,"* or *"volcanic."* The only time that may be critical data is if a *"Fused-Group"* isn't easily *dispersing*. But, in that case, it is far more *systematically effective* to *locate* (on the *map*) the *"assembly center"* where they were *fused*.

Another key to *releasing* B.E. from a heavily impactful *incident* is to *defragment* any significant specific *protest-charge* that may be *holding* their *attention* on the *incident*. This is *processed-out* just like STEP-B of the "*Standard Procedure: PME–Long Version*" (described later). The type of *fragmented-charge* will not be on "*going interior*," but another type of specific *resistive-effort* (or *counter-effort*) applied in the incident. [The basic method is "*Spotting*" the *correct item*, and *defrag-by-Awareness* "*As-It-Is*."] Assess from the following list:

"*In This Incident, Is There An Effort...*"

1. *To Stop?*

2. *To Withdraw?*

3. *To (Both) Stop And Withdraw?*

4. *Suppress Something?*

5. *Invalidate Something?*

6. *Protest About Something?*

7. *Hold Onto A Picture (Of The Incident)?*

8. *Hurry Or Rush?*

9. *To Make Something "Not Be"?*

STANDARD PROCEDURE: ENTITIES

We have already introduced the three primary techniques used for this *Standard Procedure for Entities* (*Fragments, &tc.*):

1. *Locational*

2. *Identification*

3. *Heaven Incident*

These may be worked forwards and backwards (*1-2-3-2-1-2-3..*) until a B.E. (or *Fragment, Split &tc.*) *releases*.

Combining what you've learned in this manual, let's add some additional introductory guidelines so you can put this into practice. Here are some basic steps to get you started.

A. Close your eyes and "*look*" over the *Body* and the space around the *Body* (the "shell" could extend three feet or more). You are "*looking*" for areas or spots that seem to have "pressure" or some "energetic-mass."

B. *"Get the sense"* of contacting or permeating the *"entity"* that is generating the "pressure" (or "mass").

C. Apply the *"Locational Technique"* (using information given previously in this manual). If you still sense that the presence remains, continue to STEP-D.

D. Apply the *"Identification Technique"* (using information given previously in this manual).

D1. Ask them *"What Are You?"* and sort of "feel" for an answer coming back from them. You may just get a subtle "idea" or "impression" of what they are "being." You might have to "infuse" them with a bit of life—or "enliven" them directly with your *Awareness of them being there;* "granting" them a bit more *"Beingness"* —in order to "draw out" a response. [This is simply done by focused and directed *intention.*]

D2. Ask them *"Who Are You?"* and, if necessary, steer them toward the *"Me"* answer. *Acknowledge* any responses; but the *release* generally occurs only when the *"Me"* answer is *acknowledged*. Repeat STEP-D2 until you get the *"Me"-release*. If the *entity releases (leaves/blows-off)*, continue to STEP-E; if the *entity* does not *release*, go to STEP-F.

E. Check for *"Copies."* Sometimes another *entity* will immediately *create a "Copy"* of the one that just left, or even assume its *phase* themselves. If you get a sense of this happening, *spot* that others are *copying*; then *project* (or *intend*) an *acknowledgment* to them for doing that. This usually gets them to stop; then you can *defragment/dissolve* the *"Copy"* by *Awareness/Spotting* and/or apply the *"Locational Technique"* to it, &tc.

F. Check for *"Holders."* Sometimes another *entity* will attempt to "hold onto" the one that is *releasing.* If you get a sense of this happening, *Spot* that it *Is*, and *acknowledge* the other *entity* for doing that. When the first one *releases*, you can then shift your *attention* to handling the "*Holder*." If the *entity* you are attempting to release is not being "held" by another *entity*, continue to STEP-G.

NOTE: You can shift *attention* to handle a "*Holder*" as your next *entity* to *defragment*. However, this is not usually standard practice for "*Copiers*" —unless it is a *single entity* for certain, and not a *group*; because these *entities* really like to create "*Copies*" (it is the basic skill of an *Alpha-Spirit*) and you can quickly become overwhelmed trying to handle too many *Copiers* and *Copies* at once.

G. If you run into trouble with the previous steps, are not getting any answers/responses, or otherwise are unable to get an *entity* to *release*, then apply the "*Incident-Running Technique*" specifically on the *Heaven Implant* (relying on the *sequence outline* provided in this manual, in addition to your own experience with the *incident*). Gently "push" the *entity* through the *incident*.

H. If at any time, while performing these techniques, you find your attention being drawn to anything that you get the sense of being a "*piece*" of yourself, apply the "*Locational Technique*" to it.

Communication between the *Seeker* and *entity* occurs on a "*telepathic link*." In most cases, the procedural PCL can be "intended" or "projected" to the *entity* silently. The "*Identification Technique*" works best as a written exercise. There are some practitioners that have reached the level of freely *processing entities* out loud—but when first starting out, *silent intention* works best for *focusing* on a *single* B.E., so as not to stir up others.

A *Seeker/Wizard* should handle *entities* as various "layers" become *accessible* during *upper-level* work. The *in-session* handling of *entities* may be accomplished in between treating other areas and developing *spiritual perception* (such as *A.T. Manual #6*). *Entities* become more *accessible* the longer a *Seeker* works with their *Advanced Training*. It is important to not become too obsessive about directly "searching for" or trying to "locate" *entities*; because if you "push" or "intend" too hard in a certain spot, you will frequently find yourself forcing a B.E. to occupy that location.

Self-Honesty is critical for *upper-grade* work. At *Level-8*, the insistence, expectancy, or demand of a *Wizard* that "something" *is* "there" *will put* "something" "there."

As you know, *Alpha-Spirits* are not *actually* "located" in any *space-time* "location" or position. An individual is not *actually* "*within*" the *Universe* that they are operating their *Awareness* from, but unfortunately, the *Human Condition* tends to be confined or restricted to such *considerations-of-Beingness*. However, this also applies to other *entities* (B.E., &tc.) that you encounter. They are only located by their own *consideration*; and since they are highly suggestible and you are now more *Actualized*, they can also be located by *your considerations*.

Let's examine an example of this. For training purposes: there is an *out-of-phase* B.E. that is compulsively occupying a bookshelf—*"being a bookshelf," "being in a bookshelf,"* &tc. You "touch" or "contact" the *entity* and it gets the *realization* that it's not there (and never *actually* was, except as a *consideration*) and it *"releases"* and ceases to be there.

This phenomenon occurs so quickly that you keep *trying to locate* them—and since you can *actually* "reach" your *Awareness* anywhere in *space-time* (and in *any Universe*), you can still "reach" the *entity*, and the effect is essentially relocating them back. This not only falsely *locates* the *entity* in *space-time* again, but also *invalidates* their previous *realization/release*. If this happens, all a *Seeker/Wizard* needs to do is rehabilitate the *release* by *"Spotting"* the instance that the *location was enforced*, then *release* the *entity* again (if it remains).

In this wise, a *Seeker* should beware *"pulling-in"* or even *"creating" entities to be run on processing*. This is a real phenomenon that takes place, which is why *"Entities & Fragments"* is only treated at *Level-8*. After handling of *entities* has begun, the danger comes from "blaming things" on *entities* when/if they are not the direct cause. This is the same as saying or thinking *something is there* when it isn't. This also means potentially *creating* "*things*" *to be there* that are *misidentified* as *something else*; which makes *defragmenting* it *"As-It-Is"* quite difficult later.

An individual's *inabilities* and *fragmentation* are still part of one's own case—one's own *considerations, reality-agreements* and *postulates.* This *fragmentation* can certainly be made worse, *amplified* by the presence of B.E., but they are not the ultimate "reason why" of our problems. There are other parts of *Level-8* that focus more directly on a *Seeker's* own *spiritual perception;* don't make the mistake of thinking that all *Alpha-fragmentation* and *perceived spiritual ability barriers* are being imposed exclusively from the "outside."

"PLATFORMS #1-18" (AT#3 ADDENDUM)

A *Seeker's* own *run* of "#1-18" helps break up solid blocks of *fused-entities* (and may even *release* some directly). The true purpose of *running* it at *Level-8* is to make *entities* "available" or "accessible" for *processing.* Additionally, it is a primary component of the *"Hellfire Incident"* (appearing in the *sequence* of *Implants* that were applied during that *incident*). *Implants* "#1-18" originally appeared individually at various times on the *Backtrack,* but were also eventually employed as part of heavy mass (widespread) *Implanting-Incidents.*

[The following is additional data for the "#1-18" series given in *AT#3*.]

PLATFORM #1X

The *Platform* given in *AT#3* provides a long-form using "{*electric-shock*}" as the *implanting-gimmick*. This is actually only one of *twelve* different "{*feelings*}" that this *Platform-pattern* was used for. *Run* the entire *pattern* completely on each of the following in sequence:

1. *Pleasure*; 2. *Pain*; 3. *Heat*; 4. *Cold*; 5. *Electric-Shock*; 6. *Numbness*; 7. *Sensation*; 8. *Dizziness*; 9. *Pressure*; 10. *Suction (vacuum)*; 11. *Flash (explosion)*; 12. *Blackness*.

PLATFORM #3X

The *Platform* given in *AT#3* provides a long-form using "SURVIVE" as the reoccurring *item*. This is actually only one of *ten* different reoccurring "{*implant-items*}" that this *Platform-pattern* was used for. *Run* the entire *pattern* completely on each of the following in sequence:

1. *Obey*; 2. *Rebel*; 3. *Work*; 4. *Be Lazy*; 5. *Love*; 6. *Hate*; 7. *Survive*; 8. *Die*; 9. *Create*; 10. *Destroy*.

PLATFORM #14X

The *Platform* given in *AT#3* provides a long-form using "PICTURE MACHINE" as the reoccurring *item*. This is actually only one of *seven* different "{*machine terminals*}" that this *Platform-pattern* was used for. *Run* the entire *pattern* completely on each of the following in sequence:

1. *Postulating Machine*; 2. *Picture Machine*;

3. *Thinkingness Machine*; 4. *Somatic (or Sensation) Machine*; 5. *Reality Machine*; 6. *Confusion Machine* ; 7. *Forgettingness Machine*.

PLATFORM #16B

This *Platform* is *not* given in *AT#3*. It is a short-form formula. *Run* the entire *pattern* completely on each of the following *terminals* in sequence:

1. *Treasure*; 2. *Wealth*; 3. *Love*; 4. *Knowledge*; 5. *Pleasure*; 6. *Bodies*; 7. *Glory*; 8. *Honor*; 9. *Identity*; 10. *Immortality*.

16B.0.0 **STAY**. *& Spot the Alpha*

16B.1.1x **SEEK** ___. *& Spot the Alpha*

16B.1.2x **DO NOT SEEK** ___.
& Spot the Alpha

16B.1.3x **ABANDON** ___.
& Spot the Alpha

16B.1.4x **DO NOT ABANDON** ___.
& Spot the Alpha

16B.2.1x **DISCOVER** ___.
& Spot the Alpha

16B.2.2x **DO NOT DISCOVER** ___.
& Spot the Alpha

16B.2.3X OVERLOOK ___.
& Spot the Alpha

16B.2.4X DO NOT OVERLOOK ___.
& Spot the Alpha

16B.3.1X FIND ___. *& Spot the Alpha*

16B.3.2X DO NOT FIND ___.
& Spot the Alpha

16B.3.3X MISS ___. *& Spot the Alpha*

16B.3.4X DO NOT MISS ___.
& Spot the Alpha

16B.4.1X GRAB ___. *& Spot the Alpha*

16B.4.2X DO NOT GRAB ___.
& Spot the Alpha

16B.4.3X DISCARD ___.
& Spot the Alpha

16B.4.4X DO NOT DISCARD ___.
& Spot the Alpha

16B.5.1X CLUTCH ___.
& Spot the Alpha

16B.5.2X DO NOT CLUTCH ___.
& Spot the Alpha

16B.5.3X RELEASE ___.
& Spot the Alpha

16B.5.4X DO NOT RELEASE ___.
& Spot the Alpha

16B.6.1x OBTAIN ___. *& Spot the Alpha*

16B.6.2x DO NOT OBTAIN ___.
        & Spot the Alpha

16B.6.3x DISDAIN ___.
        & Spot the Alpha

16B.6.4x DO NOT DISDAIN ___.
        & Spot the Alpha

16B.7.1x TAKE ___. *& Spot the Alpha*

16B.7.2x DO NOT TAKE ___.
        & Spot the Alpha

16B.7.3x GIVE ___. *& Spot the Alpha*

16B.7.4x DO NOT GIVE ___.
        & Spot the Alpha

16B.8.1x HAVE ___. *& Spot the Alpha*

16B.8.2x DO NOT HAVE ___.
        & Spot the Alpha

16B.8.3x GIVE UP ___.
        & Spot the Alpha

16B.8.4x DO NOT GIVE UP ___.
        & Spot the Alpha

16B.9.1x SAVE ___. *& Spot the Alpha*

16B.9.2x DO NOT SAVE ___.
        & Spot the Alpha

16B.9.3x WASTE ___. *& Spot the Alpha*

16B.9.4X **DO NOT WASTE ___.**
& Spot the Alpha

16B.10.1X **PRESERVE ___.**
& Spot the Alpha

16B.10.2X **DO NOT PRESERVE ___.**
& Spot the Alpha

16B.10.3X **DESTROY ___.**
& Spot the Alpha

16B.10.4X **DO NOT DESTROY ___.**
& Spot the Alpha

16B.11.1X **GUARD ___.** *& Spot the Alpha*

16B.11.2X **DO NOT GUARD ___.**
& Spot the Alpha

16B.11.3X **NEGLECT ___.**
& Spot the Alpha

16B.11.4X **DO NOT NEGLECT ___.**
& Spot the Alpha

16B.12.1X **SAFEGUARD ___.**
& Spot the Alpha

16B.12.2X **DO NOT SAFEGUARD ___.**
& Spot the Alpha

16B.12.3X **RISK ___.** *& Spot the Alpha*

16B.12.4X **DO NOT RISK ___.**
& Spot the Alpha

16B.13.1x PROTECT ___.
& Spot the Alpha
16B.13.2x DO NOT PROTECT ___.
& Spot the Alpha
16B.13.3x ENDANGER ___.
& Spot the Alpha
16B.13.4x DO NOT ENDANGER ___.
& Spot the Alpha
16B.14.1x EXHIBIT ___. *& Spot the Alpha*
16B.14.2x DO NOT EXHIBIT ___.
& Spot the Alpha
16B.14.3x HIDE ___. *& Spot the Alpha*
16B.14.4x DO NOT HIDE ___.
& Spot the Alpha
16B.15.1x OWN ___. *& Spot the Alpha*
16B.15.2x DO NOT OWN ___.
& Spot the Alpha
16B.15.3x DISOWN ___.
& Spot the Alpha
16B.15.4x DO NOT DISOWN ___.
& Spot the Alpha
16B.16.1x WIN ___. *& Spot the Alpha*
16B.16.2x DO NOT WIN ___.
& Spot the Alpha
16B.16.3x LOSE ___. *& Spot the Alpha*

16B.16.4X **DO NOT LOSE ___.**
& Spot the Alpha

16B.17.1X **BUY ___.** *& Spot the Alpha*

16B.17.2X **DO NOT BUY ___.**
& Spot the Alpha

16B.17.3X **SELL ___.** *& Spot the Alpha*

16B.17.4X **DO NOT SELL ___.**
& Spot the Alpha

16B.18.1X **STEAL ___.** *& Spot the Alpha*

16B.18.2X **DO NOT STEAL ___.**
& Spot the Alpha

16B.18.3X **REJECT ___.** *& Spot the Alpha*

16B.18.4X **DO NOT REJECT ___.**
& Spot the Alpha

16B.19.1X **GATHER ___.**
& Spot the Alpha

16B.19.2X **DO NOT GATHER ___.**
& Spot the Alpha

16B.19.3X **SEPARATE ___.**
& Spot the Alpha

16B.19.4X **DO NOT SEPARATE ___.**
& Spot the Alpha

16B.20.1X **REMEMBER ___.**
& Spot the Alpha

16B.20.2X **DO NOT REMEMBER ___.**
  & Spot the Alpha
16B.20.3X **FORGET ___.**
  & Spot the Alpha
16B.20.4X **DO NOT FORGET ___.**
  & Spot the Alpha
16B.21.0 **GO AWAY.** *& Spot the Alpha*

PROGRAMMED MACHINE-ENTITIES

"Spiritual Machinery" is introduced in *PC Lesson-14.* Now that we have discussed *entities* at *Level-8,* we can extend our reach further in this area. *"Simple (or Light) Machinery"*—that is directly *created* as as a *machine* or *response-circuit mechanism*—is relatively easy to *defragment.* A *Seeker* simply applies *"creativeness processes"* (*imagining copies, alteration of copies,* and the *creation* and *destruction* of *copies, &tc.*) or even the *"Standard Procedure (for Entities)"* on *Light Machinery.*

There is also more advanced *"machinery"* that consists of a *systematic series* of *programmed postulates*—or *"circuitry"*—that *creates/manifests* something, or causes something to occur. This *programming* can become quite complex—similar to *programs* and *operating systems* for *personal computers*, except that they range all the way up to the level of *creating* and *managing* entire *Universes*.

This *"programmed machine-circuitry"* can actually be quite useful, and is only mildly *fragmentary* in itself. One primary liability to their *creation* is that an *Alpha-Spirit* could set one to run forever, forget about it, and subsequently lose *responsibility* and *control* for its *creation*. Later (more recently) on the *Backtrack*, these forgotten *machines* also get "infested" by B.E. that *copy* them, and *fragment* their operation, *&tc*. This, again, can all be handled with *Standard Procedures* and even methods given for earlier *processing-levels*.

Early on the *Backtrack*, an *Alpha-Spirit* would *"imprint"* the *programming* onto some kind of *template* or *platform*. [This will be off in some separate (extra-dimensional) *Space* that you've *created* for it.] You would *knowingly* "activate" or "trigger" the *machinery* by *reaching* back and *projecting* a bit of *intention* (or *energy* in more recent *Universes*) on a communication-line (*focused attention*) toward that *template*.

Also, early on the *Backtrack*, *Alpha-Spirits* had the ability to more easily and *knowingly* "erase" each other's *machinery*. Of course, we could just *create* it again—but this led to a tendency toward making multiple *copies* of *templates* and "stacking" them behind various "levels" of *alteration* (*postulates of "It-As-Changed"*) in order to make getting at (or *destroying*) the basic *structural template* of the *machine* more difficult for others.

By the era of the *"Symbols Universe"* (*see*

AT#1), the decline of *Spiritual Awareness* resulted in too many *considerations* of *inability* (*Alpha-fragmentation*) to keep all of one's *machinery* "manifested" (in the face of persistent opposition). The solution to this was to *create* a new type of *machinery* that could *persist*. This led to the idea of *making beings* (*spirits*) into *machines*, *implanting* them to keep the *machinery* created. But, *Alpha-Spirits* were still fairly powerful *beings* during the *Symbols Universe* era, and they wouldn't stay in that *phase of Beingness* forever. At some point, the *being* would just basically say "*To hell with this*," and *release* itself.

Programmed Machine-Entities (or "PME") currently in existence primarily stem from the *Magic Universe*. During that era, "*entities*" were essentially the high-value money—such as with "*magic rings*" or "*relics*." But there are also some *entities* that were *crafted/made* into PME during this *Universe*. And by this, we mean *Al-*

pha-Spirits (and *fragments*) made into *"machine cores"* (resembling tiny *black crystalline cylinders*), which follow a series of *pre-programmed postulates* (or *"circuitry"*) laid out on a *"machine template."* PME are not operating on their own *postulates*; so don't hate on them too much (and handle them civilly).

"Implant Dealers" (from technologically advanced civilizations) are the primary manufacturers of PME in *this Universe.* This means they also serve as *"spirit collectors."* For example: after a mass (widespread) *Implant*—such as the *Hellfire Incident*—there are a lot of *fragmented pieces* of *beings* basically lying around. These are then *collected* and made into PME. The existing PME and B.E. *fragments* could also be *re-purposed.*

More recently on the *Backtrack,* one of the more modern types of PME is the *"Virus."* These are not simple *organic lifeforms,* or like other forms of *biological decay;* they were all intentionally *created*. They are usually used against enemy populations, but they are also unleashed on *"prison planets"* to suppress its inhabitants. Most of the current *viruses* on *Earth* were implanted here in the last *6,000* to *12,000 years* in order to keep the growing population of *"inmates"* under greater control (and reduce the *Human lifespan*).

A *"splitter mechanism"* is often *encoded* in PME programming. This is *systematically* referred to as a *"Split-Viewpoint"* or *"SV-Mechanism."* We are legally not permitted to even suggest using *Systemology* to attempt to *"cure"* any *viruses*—but for illustrative purposes: if you were to *process* a *virus* as a PME, you would actually find thousands of PME in the *body*. *Processing* a single one might *release* it, but it is immediately replaced by whichever is the original one, splitting again, and then reappearing in that location.

Many older PME types also have this *"re-*

placement-quality" —and you would have to work through a few "layers" of *templates* to approach the original. Some B.E. will do this, too— which can sometimes make the *entity-handling* portion of *Level-8* seem endless.

Similar to the *"Locational Procedure"* for B.E., the ultimate undercut-PCL for PME is:

"Spot Being Made Into A Machine."

Ever since its introduction during the *Symbols Universe* era, PME *construction* typically occurs within a long *cylinder*. It resembles the shape of the *"machine core"* that the *entity* is made into. The *"surface walls"* of the *cylinder* were covered in *holographic imagery* of IPU-*terminals*. The *entity* would typically have a low-level of *"confront"* on at least some of these *images* —so an increased *resistance* to *"touching the walls"* develops.

Where the *entity* would have otherwise

been able to pass through the material-surface of the *cylinder*, a *reactive-withdraw* (or "*attention flinch*") tendency is being *conditioned*. As layers of *holographic imagery* increasingly compounded, the *cylinder* is made to appear as though it were "*shrinking,*" and as a *reactive-effect*, the *entity* would also "*squeeze*" its own *considerations-of-Beingness* tighter and tighter. This is also how "*high-pressure*" *Group-Fusing Incidents* are accomplished, for which the entry-point is: "*(Spot) The Cylinder.*" The event just prior to this: you will find them being *entrapped* or *captured* in some manner.

In addition to "*Viruses,*" another PME that has appeared more recently on *Earth* in the last few thousand years is the "*Wraith.*" Although these *machines* don't really have *Human-language* names, we use the word "*Wraith*" to describe an "*energy-draining machine-entity.*" These are semi-moble; they do not attach permanently to the *Alpha-Spirit*, but once they get into a *body*, they tend to remain with it until it dies (unless they are *systematically released*).

The *"Wraith"* makes one feel *tired* and *weak*. It is possible they were originally released to accelerate *"aging"* on *Earth*. Most individuals accumulate (pick up) at least a few every year, so it makes sense that there is at least some connection. Once in the body, they are *single points* that tend to "pull in" *energy* rather than emanate it, so they are not always easy to "see." They can also move around a bit, a zig-zag within a small area, but once you can focus your *attention* on them (and track them a bit), they tend to settle down. They are easy to *release*.

There are certain types of *"mobile-machines"* that are heavily *imprinted* with *low-Awareness* misemotion, such as: *fatigue, laziness, hopelessness, apathy, &tc*. These types of *machines* tend to drift in, hang around for a while, and then move off to somewhere else. Sometimes they get stuck to your other *machinery* and can linger around an *Alpha-Spirit* for a few lifetimes. They are often perceived as *vague colored-spheres*.

"*Monitors*" or "*Watchers*" (they may give a *Meter-read* on either title) are another commonly encountered PME. They are attached to both *Alpha-Spirits* and *bodies* in order to "keep an eye" on them. A *Seeker* will likely be carrying a few from as far back as the *Magic Universe*.

The "*Monitor/Watchers*" try hard to keep hidden and simply "*watch*" ("*monitor*"). They are usually perceived "over the head" or "behind the back." Many of them are reporting to old empires and forces that don't even exist anymore and so they aren't generally troublesome. But some of them report to the more recent "*invader-forces*" about such things as your *Ascension-work* in *Systemology*, or if you successfully demonstrate the ability to *"break the game"* by *levitating an object*, or something like that.

There is also *machinery* that tries to hide other *machinery* and even inhibit or block your handling or *processing* of *machinery*. Remember that we all have a lot of *Implanting* ("Platforms #1-18") that attempt to prevent us from *dispersing, blowing,* or *defragmenting* all types of *machinery*.

There are even instances where we have each contributed a *"split-fragment"* of ourselves to a *machine* that is *installed* on someone else. There are many reasons this may have happened (civic duty, price of a magic spell, *&tc.*). There are *"splitter implants"* embedded in all 64 IPU. Most of this can simply be *Spotted* and *defragmented-by-Awareness*. [Handling *"split-viewpoints"* directly really requires a separate procedure.]

Because you are apply a *GSR-Meter* on

behalf of an *entity*, anything that involves assessing IPU *for them* can be difficult if you, yourself, still have a lot of *fragmented charge* on those *terminals*. For this reason, the material from *A.T. Manual #4* ("*Implanted Universes*") should be *defragmented* before handling too much *systematic processing* on *machinery*. The IPU reflect a more *fragmentary* part of your own personal case than all of the *machinery* that has since been accumulated.

STANDARD PROCEDURE: PME

Unlike B.E. (previously), the PME are not always so easy to "wake up" and *defragment*. They have *considered* themselves *to be machinery* for a very long time. There are really two different versions of this procedure: a *long* and a *short*.

• The *long version* treats the entire cycle of their *entrapment* in detail, and *releases* them on a simple gradient. It does, however, require a lot of *session-time* to *run*. A *Seeker* should start with this to get familiarity with all the parts of the procedure.

• Effectively applying the *short version* simply requires having a much higher-level of *Actualized Awareness*—sufficient to grant or imbue the PME with enough *Beingness* (*livingness, &tc.*) to "Spot" a couple of key things, without having to treat the other stuff on the *long version*.

Sometimes you can find the PME directly. Most of the time you just handle the "*machinery*"—which consists of the PME, the *programmed-template*, various *imprints* and *circuitry*, and usually other B.E. and *Fused-Groups*. You simply *run* the *Standard Procedure* on the whole *machine*. Most of it will *defragment* within a few steps, which leaves the "*machine core*" that you handle by completing the procedure.

Sometimes "*remnants*" will remain—

where the *"core" releases*, but a *Seeker* discovers a few days later the whole thing is apparently *created* again. You can check for a *remnant-machine-core* after the *main-core* blows-off, and continue *processing* it if it gives a *GSR-Meter "read."* [This is an *"advanced systematic GSR-Biofeedback metering procedure."*]

LONG VERSION

A. *Locate the PME.*

Locate the PME, or the *machinery* containing the PME. [The basic method is to *"focus attention"* and get *"Meter-reads"* where something *Is*, and wherever *fragmented charge* is present.] If a *machine*, check for a *Meter-read* on: "PME (?)" —because there may just be *light machinery*, which only requires B.E. procedures. If it's quite obvious to you that there is a "more basic original" *behind* what you've located, then shift your *attention* to that one.

B. *Defragment protest on "going interior."*

This is a *GSR-Meter* assessment on a list of *keywords/buttons* (similar to what is introduced in *PC Lesson-10*). PME (and *complex-machinery*) almost always have some *fragmented charge* related to at least one of these areas. The one that *"reads"* strongest is the *primary charge*. You also note and *acknowledge* when there are smaller *"reads"* on something. [The basic method is *"Spotting"* the *correct item*, and *defrag-by-Awareness "As-It-Is."*]

PME *fragmentation* on *"going interior"* may be related to *incidents* prior to being made into a *machine*; but generally *that is* the greatest *protest* (for these areas) on their *Backtrack*. In rare cases, the *"reading"* charge may be *"On"* instead of *"In"*; but this is only the case for a few PME built up in multiple layers, and the following list should suffice for most applications.

1. *Want To Go In*

2. *Can't Get In*

3. *Kicked Out (Of Spaces)*

4. *Can't Go In*

5. *Being Trapped*

6. *Forced In*

7. *Pulled In*

8. *Pushed In*

9. *Made To Go In*

10. *Made Into A Machine*

C. {optional} *Date when they went into the body.*

This is really only useful toward *defragmenting* mobile PME (*e.g.* a *Virus*) that went in relatively recently. For other *machinery* that was built, installed in you (or attached to your *beingness*) long ago, and has remained ever since: this is more of a *research action*. ["*Dates*" are determined by narrowing down a fixed time period using *Meter-reads*.]

D. "*Spot Being Made Into A Machine.*"

Have them *Spot* being *made into a machine*. [If necessary, "*Date*" and "*Locate*" it with the *GSR-Meter.*] The basic method for this is to first check *"which Universe"* it occurred in: *"This One (?); Magic Universe (?); Earlier Universe (?)."* You can also apply the *"locational"* method of having them *"point to where..."*

More recent PME were in a mass (widespread) *Implanting-Incident* prior to experiencing the *machine-building.* You can have them *Spot* this (even *"date"* and *"locate"*) and *Spot* the prior instance of *"capture"*—or whatever was the *"beginning"* of the *incident.* You may have to take some of the *charge* off of the *incident* that occurred prior to the *machine-building* in order to get the PME to confront the actual *machine-incident.*

[Only work with this step long enough to get the *machine* to start coming apart or loosening up—freeing *attention* from its *fixation* on *solidity.* Eventually a *"Wizard"* will be at a point where enough *Beingness* can be *enlivened* in the PME for it to directly *"Spot"* such things as *"being made into a machine"* with enough high-level *attention* that it will simply *defrag-by-Awareness.*]

E. *"Spot The First (Earliest) Time You Were Made Into A Machine."*

This means finding the most basic (earliest) *incident* of being made into a *machine.* In every case researched, the *incident* was found in the *Symbols Universe.* It nearly always predates the current *machinery* they are *"being."* This means that PME (and their *remnants/fragments*) have had a long history of *being a machine* of some type.

This data may not be accessible to the PME—and if so, it is likely too entangled with other *entities* and unknown factors to be properly *"dated and located"* with *Meter-reads.* The other possibility is that there are *"harmful-acts"* connected to this area, which is inhibiting their *ability-to-confront.* So, as an alternative to this step (as given), you can run the PCL: "*In The Symbols Universe, Spot Making Others Into Machines.*"

F. "*Spot Being Captured (Before Being Made Into a Machine).*"

In our original version of this procedure, it was suggested to use a list of *IPU-traps* as an assessment action, in an attempt to *systematically identify* an answer. This proved to be a long tedious (and eventually unnecessary) task. Instead, *direct their attention* earlier to the "*Implant Penalty-Universes*" (*see AT#4*) and indicate to them that these IPU are what underlie all the entrapment techniques used in the *Symbols Universe*.

G. *Assess for the Penalty-Universe underlying their entrapment.*

Use the data provided in *A.T. Manual #4*, "*Implanted Universes.*" First use a list of the *16 Dynamic Systems*, and assess for the best/strongest "*reading*" on the list. When you have one, you assess from the list of

4 *Goals* for that *Dynamic System*. Take the one that *"reads"* as the IPU-*Goal* for STEP-H. If you are dealing with a *"composite-case,"* you may have to repeat this step to *process-out* a few *Goals* (in the same or different *Dynamic Systems*) to fully *defragment* everything.

H. *IPU-Defragmentation.*

As you find each IPU-*Goal*, have the PME *run* the following PCL-sequence:

–*"Spot: 'To {Goal} Is Native State'."*

–*"Spot Being Pushed Into This."*

–and/or *"Spot Pushing Another Into This."*

–and/or *"Spot Others Pushing Others Into This."*

–*"Spot: 'To {Goal} Is Native State'."*

It may be that you need to *process-out* another PCL-*Goal* (from STEP-G). If necessary, this can be followed up with *"Who Are You?"* (from the *"Identification Procedure"*) in order to get a *"Me"* answer. The PME may or may not *defragment* at this step, or any of the other steps, from this *Standard Procedure*.

I. *Agreements-Universe Defragmentation.*

If there is still something remaining, have the PME *run* the following PCL-sequence regarding the *"Agreements Universe"* (*see AT#1, &tc.*):

−*"Spot Rushing To Get Into Agreement."*

−*"Spot Going Through 'The Inverted Golden Triangle'."*

−*"Spot: 'To Agree Is Native State'."*

−*"Look Earlier And Spot When You Decided To Agree."*

Again, this can be followed up with *"Who Are You?"* (from the *"Identification Procedure"*) in order to get a *"Me"* answer. The PME may *release* at this step, or any of the previous steps. If necessary you can also have them *"Spot Encouraging Others To Agree"* and *"Spot Others Encouraging Others To Agree."*

Running the wrong *Goal* for this procedure is not really problematic. All *Alpha-Spirits* have *some fragmented charge* on each of the *64* IPU. Sometimes you will suddenly find the *machinery* blow apart into a cloud of *individuals* — you *acknowledge* them and handle each of the partial-*releases* one by one. We have also found that if you take a break at a time like this, some of them just seem to sort their stuff out and blow off. You can then check back later and see if some require more *defragmentation processing,* or whether there is still a *core-remnant* that still needs to be *processed-out.*

Elements of *"Standard Procedure: Entities"* also applies to PME (it just usually isn't enough for handling PME without some of the steps given above). This means having to check for *"Holders"* and *"Copiers/Copies."* One *machine* may be trying to "hold" or "hide" another. There may even be a *"repair-machine"* that keeps the *machine* you are *processing* in place or copies it when it leaves. Simply check for this stuff and handle it.

SHORT VERSION

This is a shorter script but a more advanced version of the above procedure. It relies on the *high-Awareness level* of a "Wizard" to grant enough *Beingness* or *livingness* to the PME, that it raises the *entity's Awareness* high enough to simply "*Spot*" critical *items* with their *attention* and "*defrag-by-Awareness.*"

This is the preferred *A.T. version*. With enough *practice/certainty*, it may even be operated *out-of-session*—once a "Wizard" has learned how to apply the entirety of *Systemology without Biofeedback-Devices* (which is an important skill-set for when you find yourself free of your body and material objects).

As you are still developing skill, this is best practiced on a *GSR-Meter*. You should get "*reads*" on each step and get a sense for *machinery* gradually "coming apart" or *releasing*. It follows the same formula as the *"Long Version,"* which a *"Wizard"* should get familiar with first.

A. *Locate the machine.*

It will *read* on: "PME" or *"machine."*

B. *"Spot Being Made Into A Machine."*

It should considerably loosen up with this step (though not always as much as STEP-D of the *Long Version*). If necessary, you can *"date and locate"* (anything from STEP-B to D of the *Long Version*). But really, this step can be accomplished by simple *"Spotting"*—if you can endow the *being* with enough *livingness* to overcome their reactive and conditioned *flinch/withdrawal* from the *"time and location"* of the *incident*.

C. *"Spot The First (Earliest) Time You Were Made Into A Machine."*

This is the same as STEP-E from the *Long Version*. However, in the *Long Version*, you can get away with being a little vague, whereas here, this must be *Spotted* by the PME with high certainty in order to *defrag-by-Awareness*.

D. *"Spot Making Others Into Machines."*

Run the PCL.

E. *"Spot Being Tricked Into Thinking That Machines Are Necessary."*

If the *entity/machinery* remains, continue.

F. *Identification.*

Run the *"Who Are You?"* PCL from the *Identification Procedure.* You may have to get them to affirm *"Me"* (and you *acknowledge* it) several times in order to *release.* Sometimes, the *release* occurs prior to this step. If they don't *release* on this, the assessment steps from the *Long Version* are too lengthy, but you can treat *"Agreements"* in the next step (if necessary).

G. *Agreements-Universe Defragmentation.*

This is the same as STEP-I from the *Long*

Version. Have the PME *run* the following PCL-sequence:

–*"Spot Rushing To Get Into Agreement."*

–*"Spot Going Through 'The Inverted Golden Triangle'."*

–*"Spot: 'To Agree Is Native State'."*

–*"Look Earlier And Spot When You Decided To Agree."*

Again, this can be followed up with *"Who Are You?"* (from the *"Identification Procedure"*) in order to get a *"Me"* answer. The PME may *release* at this step, or any of the previous steps. If necessary, you can also have them *"Spot Encouraging Others To Agree"* and *"Spot Others Encouraging Others To Agree."*

ADVANCED ENTITY-HANDLING

Most *fragments* may be *systematically* handled with the same *"Standard Proced-*

ure (for Entities)." Here, we will apply a basic exercise to increase your own *reality* on this—and which also applies to *actual handling.*

1. *Close your eyes.*

2. *"Imagine"* (*by visualization*) or *"get the sense of"* a *viewpoint* of "looking over someone's shoulder."

3. *Get a sense* of *being* there to "keep them human." [You may or may not get an *actual impression* of environmental scenery, or of someone below you.]

4. Whatever part of yourself you are *projecting* to accomplish this: direct to *it* (the PCL) *"point to the being you divided from."* [At which point it should *defragment/dissolve.*]

5. If any connectivity remains, or seems to linger in the area, alternate applying the *"Who Are You?"* (from the *"Identification Technique"*) and the *"Locational Technique"* until it fully *defragments/disperses.*

Understand that you, as an *Alpha-Spirit*, have the ability to place a *viewpoint* anywhere in *space-time* and perceive *anything*. Therefore, it is possible to continue *perceiving* or "looking at" an area even after *releasing* any *fragments* fixedly located there. One purpose of *Alpha-Defragmentation* is to regain full *conscious control* over such *viewpoints*—nothing should be "fixedly holding" our attention anywhere, or enforcing perceptions from anywhere on "automatic."

Repeat the exercise using many different people—alternating *real* (one's you know) and *imagined*—until it seems like there are no more *"real"* ones to treat in this manner. Then apply the same exercise; but this time, *get a sense* of being a particular *"body-part"* on someone else, and *being* there to "keep it solid; keep it human."

CONTROL ENTITIES (C.E.)

"Control Entities" (or *"C.E."*) are active, semi-*aware* (intelligent) *entities*, *implanted* (or *installed*) for the explicit purpose of "keeping an *Alpha-Spirit* imprisoned and/or controlled." They are quite challenging to *release* using *"Standard Procedure (for Entities)"* and they don't respond any better with PME-type handling. They are intentionally *implanted* to be *"Jailers,"* or to block *spiritual perception* (*ability*), or to keep you from *thinking about* or *knowing* certain things, &tc.

From the perspective of the C.E., they aren't doing anything *wrong*. In fact, quite the opposite, which is why they are more difficult to *release*. They actively *know* what they are doing, but they are under the delusion that they are just being "honest citizens" doing their respective duty. They were *implanted* with this *false-fragmentary data* and forced to "*split-off*" a *fragment/piece* of themselves to further *im-*

128

plant a *"imprisoned entity"* (to keep them *entrapped* and *under control*).

C.E. are most easily perceived at the *existence-level* or *reality-level* of the *"Astral Body"* (from the *Magic Universe*)—which means a *Seeker* must shift their *attention-Awareness* "up and sideways" to *perceive* (*get a sense of*) a *non-physical dimension*. [This is somewhat always the case, but we are referring to a *perceived layer* of our *Beingness* that extends to a former version of *"bodily-identity."*]

There have been C.E. in use for many layers of *Universes* extending on the *Backtrack*. They are *implanted* (or *installed*) at one level (*Universe*) in order to aid in keeping an *Alpha-Spirit* confined to a *lower level* (*Universe*). At any rate, the C.E. (themselves) believe they are "blocking" you for good orderly reasons—which means they are resistant to *defragmentation* unless you first get them to *Spot* the point of being *implanted* with *false data* (*e.g.* a *fragmented purpose*).

Until earlier procedures (in this manual) were standardized, *advanced Seekers* had no formal method for handling C.E. directly. This refined synthesis of *Level-8* (presented in the "*Keys to the Kingdom*" series) now includes an effective procedure for this, relying on a *Seeker's* experience with the other techniques given. Note that in addition to *processing-out* C.E. that are affixed to and blocking you, this procedure can also be extended to include *releasing "split-fragments"* of yourself (where you are being a C.E. to someone else).

STANDARD PROCEDURE: C.E.

A. "*Spot Being Made Into A Control Entity (or C.E.)*."

B. *Spotting the Goal.*

As a *listing/assessing* action, use PCL:

  "*Made To Split To Save Society?*"

if no read,

"*Made To Split To Gain Something?*"

if no read,

"*Made To Split To Serve A Higher Purpose?*"

C. "*Spot Being Implanted With False Data.*"

if no read (wrong wording),

"*Spot Being Implanted With A False Purpose.*"

if no read (wrong wording),

"*Spot Being Implanted With Fragmented Data.*"

if no read (wrong wording),

"*Spot Being Implanted With A Fragmented Purpose.*"

if still no read, try a different "circuit":

"*Spot Implanting Others With False Data*" (*&tc.*)

or

"*Spot Making Others Into Control Entities.*"

D. *"Spot The First Time You Were Implanted With False Data."*

Note that if the *"Meter-read"* occurred on different *"wording"* for *"False Data"* from STEP-C, then use that instead. You may also have to *"steer"* *attention* of the C.E. to a *"False Jewel"* incident—something similar to *"The Jewel"* for *this Universe*, but occurring several layers of *Universe* ago.

E. *Locational Technique.*

"Point To The Being You Divided From."

F. *Identification Technique.*

"Who Are You?" (*"Me"*)

If necessary, you can alternate between STEP-E and STEP-F toward a *release*.

G. *IPU-Defrag. {if necessary}*

If the C.E. showed up (was perceived) while handling *Implanted Penalty-Universes*, and it has not *released* from the former steps, have it *"Spot"* the top of the *Implant-Platform* for that IPU-*Goal*:

"To {Goal} Is Native State."

H. *Agreements. {if necessary}*

Although it is rarely needed, if more handling is required (the C.E. is loosened up and seems ready to *release*, but still seems to be waiting for something)— have the C.E. *run* the following PCL-sequence:

–"*Spot Rushing To Get Into Agreement.*"

–"*Spot Going Through 'The Inverted Golden Triangle'.*"

–"*Spot: 'To Agree Is Native State'.*"

–"*Spot An Earlier Decision To Agree.*"

END-POINTS & REALIZATIONS

As a *Seeker* increases their *certainty* for handling *entities* and *fragments*, they may come to the *realization* that they are reaching a point of being greater *"cause over spiritual life."* This is one of the primary purposes for introducing this manual at this point of one's *Advanced Training*.

However, it is important that once this *realization* is *actualized* in practice, that a *Seeker* does not focus too hard on treating endless *sessions* on *entities*, exclusive to all other practices. This means that the presence of *"more entities"* should not hinder a *Seeker* in continuing their *Advanced Training* with *A.T. Manual #6, "Spiritual Perception."*

In fact, a *Seeker* is likely to achieve greater, more stable, gains in progress by: shifting *attention* between practicing exercises to increase *spiritual perception* –and– *processing-sessions* directed toward *entities*. As one's *spiritual perception* improves, so to will their ability to *locate* and *release* any *entities* and *fragments*.

In addition to the *entities* and *spiritual fragments* of others that "cling" to us and hold us in the *Human Condition*, the majority of an individual's difficulties stem from their own *spiritual fragmentation*. By this, we mean our own *fragments*, *pieces*, and *"split viewpoints"* that are a part of the *machinery*, or act as *entities*, holding other *Alpha-Spirit's* in the *Human Condition*.

The *Locational Procedure* was originally developed to handle these *"split-viewpoints"* (or *"S.V."*). Since an *Alpha-Spirit* is not truly *located* in *space-time* except by *consideration of viewpoints*, it is quite easy to be operating from multiple *viewpoints* that are *located* separately in *space-time*.

Early on the *Backtrack,* operating from multiple *viewpoints* simultaneously was simply a basic *godlike* skill used to *knowingly animate* one's own *creations* (*Home Universe*)—and it was not very *fragmentary.* At that stage, we were quite capable of consciously extending (or *projecting*) various *remote viewpoints* and then *knowingly dispersing* them or *disconnecting.*

The *fragmentation* occurred when S.V. were enforced (or even used as payment for "magical services") and then we were blocked from consciously operating or controlling them. This greatly contributed to our decline of *spiritual ability,* and the dampening of our total *Actualized Awareness.*

There are numerous *Implanting-Incidents* that forced an individual to divide. This was the case with the *Hellfire Incident.* In the more distant past, we have seen evidence of this in the original *Implanted Penalty-Universes.* This type of *fragmented*

Awareness is what we will continue to *de-fragment* and *reclaim* as our own throughout *Level-8*.

Let's finish this unit/manual of instruction with a basic *objective exercise* to increase your *spiritual perception* and understanding of *handling entities* and *fragments*. This is done in a public place where there are many people.

1. *Spot a person*.

2. Alternate between *getting a sense of* "keeping them human" and "leaving them free."

3. When you have done this to a point of satisfaction with one person, repeat with different one.

Then practice this exercise by applying the other *"circuits"* —*getting the idea* of *others* alternately "keeping *you* human" and "leaving *you* free"; then with *others* alternately "keeping *others* human" and "leaving *others* free." Once you have com-

pleted this, in your next *subjective session,*
see if any additional *entities* and *fragments*
are now accessible.

To truly be a *"Wizard,"* a *Seeker* must
eventually reach a point where they are
no longer influenced, blocked, or held
back, by B.E.; and to where they (themselves) are no longer holding others in
the *Human Condition.* This is the essence
of *Alpha-Defragmentation*—and the first
major *upper-level* step toward regaining
one's own true and original *spiritual perception* and *ability.*

Your next Advanced Training manual is:
"Spiritual Perception"

BASIC SYSTEMOLOGY GLOSSARY

actualization : to make actual, not just potential; to bring into full solid Reality; to realize fully in *Awareness* as a "thing."

agreement (reality) : unanimity of opinion of what is "thought" to be known; an accepted arrangement of how things are; things we consider as "real" or as an "is" of "reality"; a consensus of what is real as made by standard-issue (common) participants; what an individual contributes to or accepts as "real"; in *Systemology*, a synonym for "*reality.*"

alpha : the first, primary, basic, superior or beginning of some form; in *Systemology*, referring to the state of existence operating on spiritual archetypes and postulates, will and intention "exterior" to the low-level condensation and solidarity of energy and matter as the 'physical universe' (*beta*).

alpha-spirit : a "spiritual" *Life*-form; the "true" *Self* or I-AM; the *individual*; the spiritual (*alpha*) *Self* that is animating the (*beta*) physical body or "*genetic vehicle*" using a continuous *Lifeline* of spiritual ("*ZU*") energy; an individual spiritual (*alpha*) entity possessing no physical mass or measurable waveform (motion) in the Physical Universe as itself, so it animates the (*beta*) physical body or "*genetic vehicle*" as a catalyst to experience *Self*-determined causality in effect within the *Physical Universe*; a singular unit or point of *Spiritual Awareness* that is *Aware* that it is *Aware.*

alpha thought : the highest spiritual *Self-determination* over creation and existence exercised by an Alpha-Spirit; the Alpha range of pure *Creative Ability* based on direct postulates and considerations of *Beingness*; spiritual qualities comparable to "thought" but originating in Alpha-existence, independently superior to a Mind-System.

ascension : actualized *Awareness* elevated to the point of true "spiritual existence" exterior to *beta existence*. An "Ascended Master" is one who has returned to an incarnation on Earth as an inherently *Enlightened One*, demonstrable in their words and actions; they have the ability to *Self-direct* the "Mind" and "Body" as *Self* (as a "Spirit"); and to maintain consciousness as a personal identity continuum with the same *Self-directed* control and communication of Will-Intention that is exercised, actualized and developed deliberately during one's present incarnation.

associative knowledge : significance or meaning of a facet or aspect assigned to (or considered to have) a direct relationship with another facet; to connect or relate ideas or facets of existence with one another; in traditional systems logic, an equivalency of significance or meaning between facets or sets that are grouped together, such as in *(a + b) + c = a + (b + c)*; in Systemology, erroneous associative knowledge is assignment of the same value to all facets or parts considered as related (even when they are not actually so), such as in *a = a, b = a, c = a* and so forth without distinction.

attention : active use of *Awareness* toward a specific aspect or thing; the act of "attending" with the presence of *Self*; a direction of focus or concentration of *Awareness* along a particular channel or conduit or toward a particular terminal node or communication termination point; the Self-directed concentration of personal energy as a combination of observation, thought-waves and consideration; focused application of *Self-Directed Awareness*.

awareness : the highest sense of-and-as *Self* in knowing and being as I-AM (the *Alpha-Spirit*); the extent of beingness directed as a viewpoint (POV) experienced by *Self* as *Knowingness*.

beta (awareness) : all consciousness activity ("*Awareness*") in the "Physical Universe" (KI, in *Zuism*) or else in *beta-existence*; *Awareness* within the range of the *genetic-body*, including material thoughts, emotional responses and physical motors; personal *Awareness* of physical energy and physical matter moving through physical space and experienced as "time"; the *Awareness* held by *Self* that is restricted to an organic *Lifeform* or "*genetic vehicle*" in which it experiences causality in *beta-existence*.

beta (existence) : all manifestation in the "Physical Universe" (KI, in *Zuism*); the conditions of *Awareness* for the *Alpha-spirit* (*Self*) as a physical organic *Lifeform* or "*genetic vehicle*" in which it experiences causality in the *Physical Universe*.

charge : to fill or furnish with a quality; to supply with energy; to lay a command upon; in *Systemology*—to imbue with intention; to overspread with emotion; personal energy stores and significances entwined as fragmentation in mental images, reactive-response encoding and intellectual (and/or) programmed beliefs.

channel : a specific stream, course, current, direction or route; to form or cut a groove or ridge or otherwise guide along a specific course; a direct path; an artificial aqueduct created to connect two water bodies or water or make travel possible.

circuit : a circular path or loop; a closed-path within a system that allows a flow; a pattern or action or wave movement that follows a specific route or potential path only; in *Systemology*, "*communication processing*" pertaining to a specific *flow* of energy or information along a channel; "*feedback loop.*"

communication : successful transmission of information, data, energy (&tc.) along a message line, with a reception of feedback; an energetic flow of intention to cause an effect (or duplication) at a distance; the personal energy moved or acted upon by will or else 'selective directed attention'; the 'messenger action' used to transmit and receive energy across a medium; also relay of energy, a message or signal—or even locating a personal POV (viewpoint) for the Self—along the *ZU-line*.

condense (condensation) : the transition of vapor to liquid; denoting a change in state to a more substantial or solid condition; leading to a more compact or solid form.

confront : to come around in front of; to be in the presence of; to stand in front of, or in the face of; to meet "face-to-face" or "face-up-to"; additionally, in *Systemology*, to fully tolerate or acceptably withstand an encounter with a particular manifestation without an automatic reactive response.

consideration : careful analytical reflection of all aspects; deliberation; determining the significance of a "thing" in relation to similarity or dissimilarity to other "things"; evaluation of facts and importance of certain facts; thorough examination of all aspects related to, or important for, making a decision; the analysis of consequences and estimation of significance when making decisions; also in *Systemology*, the *postulate* or *Alpha-Thought* that defines the state of *beingness* for what something "*is.*"

defragmentation : the *reparation* of wholeness; collecting all dispersed parts to reform an original whole; a process of removing "*fragmentation*" in data or knowledge to provide a clear understanding; applying techniques and processes that promote a *holistic* interconnected *alpha* state, favoring observational *Awareness* of continuity in all spiritual and physical systems; in *Systemology*, a "*Seeker*" achieving actualized "*Self-Honest Awareness*" is said to be in a basic state of *beta-defragmentation*, whereas *Alpha-defragmentation* is the rehabilitation of the *creative ability*, managing the *Spiritual Timeline* and the POV of *Self* as Alpha-Spirit (I-AM).

existence : the *state* or fact of *apparent manifestation*; the resulting combination of the Principles of Manifestation: consciousness, motion and substance; continued *survival*; that which independently exists.

exterior : outside of; on the outside; in *Systemology*, we mean specifically the POV of *Self* that is *'outside of'* the *Human Condition,* free of the physical and mental trappings of the Physical Universe; a metahuman range of consideration; see also *'Zu-Vision'*.

external : a force coming from outside; information received from outside sources; in *Systemology*, the objective *'Physical Universe'* existence, or *beta-existence*, that the Physical Body or *genetic vehicle* is essentially *anchored* to for its considerations of locational space-time as a dimension or POV.

fragmentation : breaking into parts and scattering the pieces; the *fractioning* of wholeness or the *fracture* of a holistic interconnected *alpha* state, favoring observational *Awareness* of perceived connectivity between parts; *discontinuity*; separation of a totality into parts; in *Systemology*, a person outside of *Self-Honesty* is said to be operating from a *fragmented* state.

flow : movement across (or through) a channel (or conduit); a direction of active energetic motion, typically distinguished as either an *in-flow*, *out-flow* or *cross-flow*.

genetic-vehicle : a physical *Life*-form; the physical (*beta*) body that is animated/controlled by the (*Alpha*) *Spirit* using a continuous *Spiritual Lifeline* (ZU); a physical (*beta*) organic receptacle and catalyst for the (*Alpha*) *Self* to operate "causes" and experience "effects" within the *Physical Universe*.

harmful-act : a counter-survival mode of behavior or action (esp. that causes harm to one of more *Spheres of Existence*)—or—an overtly aggressive (hostile and/or destructive) action against an individual or any other *Sphere of Existence*; in *Utilitarian Systemology*—a shortsighted (serves fewest/lowest *Spheres of Existence*) intentional overtly harmful action to resolve a perceived problem; a revision of the rule for standard *Utilitarianism* for Systemology to distinguish actions which provide the least benefit to the least number of *Spheres of Existence*, or else the greatest harm to the greatest number of *Spheres of Existence*; in *moral philosophy*—an action which can be experienced by few and/or which one would not be willing to experience for themselves (*theft, slander, rape, &tc*); an iniquity or iniquitous act.

hold-back : withheld communications (esp. actions) such as "*Hold-Outs*"; intentional (or automatic) withdrawal (as opposed to reach); Self-restraint (which may eventually be enforced or automated); not reaching, acting or expressing, when one should be; an ability that is now restrained (on automatic) due to inability to withhold it on Self-determinism alone.

hold-outs : in photography, the numerous snap-shots/pictures withheld from the final display or professional presentation of the event; withheld communications; in Utilitarian Systemology—energetic withdrawal and communication breaks with a "*terminal*" and its *Sphere of Existence* as a result of a "*Harmful-Act*"; unspoken or undiscovered (hidden, covert) actions that an individual withholds communications of, fearing punishment or endangerment of *Self-preservation* (*First Sphere*); the act of hiding (or keeping hidden) the truth of a "*Harmful-Act*"; a refusal to communicate with a *Pilot*; also "*Hold-Back.*"

holistic : the examination of interconnected systems as encompassing something greater than the *sum* of their "parts."

Human Condition : a standard default state of Human experience that is generally accepted to be the extent of its potential identity (*beingness*) —currently treated as *Homo Sapiens Sapiens,* but which is scheduled for replacement by *Homo Novus* (the "New Human").

imagination : ability to create *mental imagery* in one's Personal Universe at will and change or alter it as desired; the ability to create, change and dissolve mental images on command or as an act of will; to create a mental image or have associated imagery displayed (or "conjured") in the mind that may or may not be treated as real (or memory recall) and may or may not accurately duplicate objective reality; to employ *creative abilities* of the Spirit that are independent of reality agreements with beta-existence.

imprint : to strongly impress, stamp, mark (or outline) onto a softer 'impressible' substance; to mark with pressure onto a surface; in *Systemology*, used to indicate permanent Reality impressions marked by frequencies, energies or interactions experienced during periods of emotional distress, pain, unconsciousness, loss, enforcement, or something antagonistic to physical (personal) survival, all of which are are stored with other reactive response-mechanisms at lower-levels of *Awareness* as opposed to the active memory database and proactive processing center of the Mind; an experiential "memory-set" that may later resurface—be triggered or stimulated artificially—as Reality, of which similar responses will be engaged automatically; holographic-like imagery "stamped" onto consciousness as composed of energetic *facets* tied to the "snap-shot" of an experience.

imprinting incident : the first or original event

instance communicated and *emotionally encoded* onto an individual's "*Spiritual Timeline*" (recorded memory from all lifetimes), which formed a permanent impression that is later used to mechanistically treat future contact on that channel; the first or original occurrence of some particular *facet* or mental image related to a certain type of *encoded response*, such as pain and discomfort, losses and victimization, and even the acts that we have taken against others along the *Spiritual Timeline* of our existence that caused them to also be *Imprinted*.

intention : directed application of Will; to intend (have "in Mind") or signify (give "significance" to) for or toward a particular purpose; in *Systemology* (from the *Standard Model*)—the spiritual activity at WILL (5.0) directed by an *Alpha Spirit* (7.0); the application of WILL as "Cause" from a higher order of Alpha Thought and consideration (6.0).

interior : inside of; on the inside; in *Systemology*, we mean specifically the POV of *Self* that is fixed to the *'internal' Human Condition,* including the *Reactive Control Center* (RCC) and Mind-System or *Master Control Center* (MCC); within *beta-existence*.

internal : a force coming from inside; information received from inside sources; in *Systemology*, the objective experience of *beta-existence* associated with the Physical Body or *genetic vehicle* and its POV regarding sensation and perception; from inside the body; in the body.

invalidate : decrease the level or degree or *agreement* as Reality.

mental image : a subjectively experienced "picture" created and imagined into being by the Alpha-Spirit (or at lower levels, one of its automated mechanisms) that includes all perceptible *facets* of totally immersive scene, which may be forms originated by an individual, or a "facsimile-copy" ("snap-shot") of something seen or encountered; a duplication of wave-forms in one's Personal Universe as a "picture" that mirror an "external" Universe experience, such as an *Imprint*.

perception : internalized processing of data received by the *senses*; to become *Aware of* via the senses.

pilot : a professional steersman responsible for healthy functional operation of a ship toward a specific destination; in *Systemology*, an intensive trained individual qualified to specially apply *Systemology Processing* to assist other *Seekers* on the *Pathway*.

point-of-view (POV) : a point to view from; an opinion or attitude as expressed from a specific identity-phase; a specific standpoint or vantage-point; a definitive manner of consideration specific to an individual phase or identity; a place or position affording a specific view or vantage; circumstances and programming of an individual that is conducive to a particular response, consideration or belief-set (paradigm); a position (consideration) or place (location) that provides a specific view or perspective (subjective) on experience (of the objective).

postulate : to put forward as truth; to suggest or assume an existence *to be*; to state or affirm the existence of particular conditions; to provide a basis of reasoning and belief; a basic theory accepted as fact; in *Systemology*, Alpha-Thought —the top-most decisions or considerations made by the Alpha-Spirit regarding the "*is-ness*" (what things "are") about energy-matter and space-time.

presence : a quality of some thing (*energy/matter*) being "present" in space-time; personal orientation of *Self* as an *Awareness* (*POV*) located in present space-time (environment) and communicating with extant energy-matter.

processing command line (PCL) : a directed input; a specific command using highly selective language for *Systemology Processing*; a predetermined directive statement (cause) intended to focus concentrated attention (effect).

processing, systematic : the inner-workings or "through-put" result of systems; in *Systemology*, a method of applied spiritual technology used toward personal Self-Actualization; methods of selective directed attention, communicated language and associative imagery that increases personal control of the human condition.

realization : the clear perception of an understanding; a consideration or understanding on what is "actual"; to make "real" or give "reality" to so as to grant a property of "beingness" or "being as it is"; the state or instance of coming to an *Awareness*; in *Systemology*, "gnosis" or true knowledge achieved during *systematic processing*; achievement of a new (or higher) cognition, true knowledge or perception of Self; a consideration of reality or assignment of meaning.

responsibility : the *ability* to *respond*; the extent of mobilizing *power* and *understanding* an individual maintains as *Awareness* to enact *change*; the proactive ability to *Self-direct* and make decisions independent of an outside authority.

Seeker : an individual on the *Pathway to Self-Honesty*; a practitioner of *Mardukite Systemology* or *Systemology Processing*, that is working toward *Spiritual Ascension*.

Self-actualization : bringing the full potential of the Human spirit into Reality; expressing full capabilities and creativeness of the *Alpha-Spirit*.

Self-determinism : the freedom to act, clear of external control or influence; the personal control of Will to direct intention.

Self-honesty : the basic or original *alpha* state of *being* and *knowing*; clear and present total *Awareness* of-and-as *Self*, in its most basic and true proactive expression of itself as *Spirit* or *I-AM*—free of artificial attachments, perceptive filters and other emotionally-reactive or mentally-conditioned programming imposed on the human condition by the systematized physical world; the ability to experience existence without judgment.

spiritual timeline : a continuous stream of moment-to-moment *Mental Images* (or a record of experiences) that defines the "past" of a spiritual being (or *Alpha-Spirit*) and which includes impressions (*imprints, &tc.*) from all life-incarnations and significant spiritual events the being has encountered; in Systemology, also "*backtrack.*"

Spheres of Existence : a series of *eight* concentric circles, rings or spheres (each larger than the former) that is overlaid onto the Standard Model of Beta-Existence to demonstrate the dynamic systems of existence extending out from the POV of Self (often as a "body") at the *First Sphere*; these are given in the basic eightfold systems as: *Self, Home/Family, Groups, Humanity, Life on Earth, Physical Universe, Spiritual Universe* and *Infinity-Divinity.*

Systemology : a modern tradition of applied religious philosophy and spiritual technology based on *Arcane Tablets* (in combination with "*general systemology*" and "*games theory*") developed in the New Age underground by Joshua Free in 2011 as an advanced futurist extension of the *Mardukite Research Org.*

terminal (node) : a point, end, or mass, on a line; a connection point for closing an electric circuit, such as a post on a battery terminating at each end of its own systematic function; a point of connectivity with other points; in systems, a contact point of interaction; a point of interaction with other points.

turbulence : a quality or state of distortion or disturbance that creates irregularity of a flow or pattern; the quality or state of aberration on a line (such as ragged edges) or the emotional "turbulent feelings" attached to a particular flow or terminal node; a violent, haphazard or disharmonious commotion (such as in the ebb of gusts and lulls of wind action).

validation : a reinforcement of agreements or considerations as being "real."

viewpoint : see *"point-of-view" (POV)*.

willingness : the state of conscious Self-determined ability and interest (directed attention) to *Be*, *Do* or *Have*; a Self-determined consideration to reach, face up to (*confront*) or manage some "mass" or energy; the extent to which an individual considers themselves able to participate, act or communicate along some line, to put attention or intention on the line, or to produce (create) an effect.

ZU : the ancient Sumerian cuneiform sign for the archaic verb—*"to know," "knowingness"* or *"awareness"*; in *Mardukite Zuism and Systemology*, the active energy/matter of the "Spiritual Universe" (AN) experienced as a *Lifeforce* or *consciousness* that imbues living forms extant in the "Physical Universe" (KI); *"Spiritual Life Energy"*; energy demonstrated by the WILL of an actualized *Alpha-Spirit* in the "Spiritual Universe" (AN), which impinges its *Awareness* into the Physical Universe (KI), animating/controlling *Life* for its experience of *beta-existence* along an individual Alpha-Spirit's personal *Identity-continuum*, called a *ZU-line*.

Zu-Line : a theoretical construct in *Mardukite Zuism and Systemology* demonstrating *Spiritual*

Life Energy (*ZU*) as a personal individual "continuum" of Awareness interacting with all Spheres of Existence on the Standard Model of Systemology; a spectrum of potential variations and interactions of a monistic continuum or singular *Spiritual Life Energy* demonstrated on the Standard Model; an energetic channel of potential POV and "locations" of Beingness, demonstrated in early Systemology materials as an individual Alpha-Spirit's personal *Identity- continuum*, potentially connecting *Awareness* of *Self* with "*Infinity*" simultaneous with all points considered in existence; a symbolic demonstration of the "*Life-line*" on which *Awareness (ZU)* extends from the direction of the "Spiritual Universe" (AN) in its true original *alpha state* through an entire possible range of activity resulting in its *beta state* and control of a *genetic-entity* occupying the *Physical Universe (KI)*.

Zu-Vision : the true and basic (*Alpha*) Point-of-View (perspective, POV) maintained by *Self* as *Alpha-Spirit* outside boundaries or considerations of the *Human Condition* and *exterior* to beta-existence reality agreements with the Physical Universe; a POV of Self *as* "a unit of Spiritual Awareness" that exists independent of a "body" and entrapment in a *Human Condition*; "spirit vision" in its truest sense.

157

Collector's Edition Hardcover

THE FUNDAMENTALS OF
SYSTEMOLOGY

A Basic Course developed by
Joshua Free

*collecting material of six lesson-booklets
together in one volume!*

"Being More Than Human"

"Realities in Agreement"

"Windows To Experience"

"Ancient Systemology"

"A History of Systemology"

"Systemology Processing"

All *six* lesson-booklets of the first official
Basic Course on Mardukite Systemology
are combined together in *one volume* as
"Fundamentals of Systemology."

Lesson booklets are also available individually!

Collector's Edition Hardcover

THE PATHWAY TO
ASCENSION

The Systemology
Professional Course by
Joshua Free

All sixteen lessons available in two volumes!

"Increasing Awareness"

"Thought & Emotion"

"Clear Communication"

"Handling Humanity"

"Free Your Spirit"

"Escaping Spirit-Traps"

"Eliminating Barriers"

"Conquest of Illusion"

...and more!

All *sixteen* lesson-booklets of the newest
Professional Course on Mardukite Systemology
are combined together in *two volumes* as
"The Pathway to Ascension."

Lesson booklets are also available individually!

THE SYSTEM

Seekers and students of the *Professional Course* and *Advanced Training Course* will also be interested in the original *Systemology Core Research Series*. These 8 volumes are a complete chronological record of *Mardukite NexGen New Thought* developments published by the *Systemology Society* from 2019 through 2023.

The Systemology Core series begins with the first professional publication released when our *Mardukite Systemology* emerged from the underground in 2019, with: *"The Tablets of Destiny Revelation."*

OLOGY CORE

The Tablets of Destiny Revelation:
*How Long-Lost Anunnaki Wisdom
Can Change the Fate of Humanity*

Crystal Clear: *Handbook for Seekers*

Metahuman Destinations (*2 volumes*)

Imaginomicon:
Approaching Gateways to Higher Universes

Way of the Wizard: *Utilitarian Systemology*

Systemology-180: *Fast-Track to Ascension*

Systemology Backtrack:
Reclaiming Spiritual Power & Past-Life Memory

PUBLISHED BY THE **JOSHUA FREE** IMPRINT REPRESENTING

The Mardukite Academy of Systemology

THE JOSHUA FREE IMPRINT
JFI PUBLICATIONS

MARDUKITE
ZUISM

mardukite.com